A Genealogy Ad

From the
Garden of Eden to
Plymouth Rock

Chronicling the journey of George Soule and Mary Beckett's forefathers through history and into New England

by Theodore Parker Burbank

i

Forward

How can we possibly go back so far in time? Is this information true and accurate?

Modern technology is wonderful. The computer along with the Internet, Google, Ancestry.com and countless other resources provides instant access to records of all kinds. Birth, marriage, death, census and all sorts of other data is within easy reach of those who are interested enough and have the time to pursue it.

How can one go back so far you ask? The answer is in two parts:

Royalty

First, records regarding royalty have been kept since the beginning of recorded time.

Information regarding the birth, marriage, death and life activities of Kings, Queens, Pharaohs and the like are available back to times before the Christian Era. Such information for the Blacksmith, Baker, and Farmer etc. are scarce back more than a few generations.

The Bible plus Greek and Roman Mythology

Second, the Bible is an historical record not usually thought of as a genealogy research resource. Wasn't I surprised when I ran into Noah and shortly later, Adam and Eve when researching my roots.

Greek and Roman mythology it surprised me to discover, is another genealogy resource. Again I was shocked when following my line through these records I found myself related to ancient Greek and Roman "gods."

Apparently, many kings declared themselves gods and, as they were the king, who was there to dispute them? Certainly not the pagans of the day.

George Soule and Mary Beckett Soule are on my family tree and I'm pleased to be able to share my findings with you. Hope you will enjoy.

Disclaimer

I must admit that I am an amateur at this genealogy business and therefore one should use the material primarily for entertainment and not as a research tool. Even though I have obtained the information contained here from respected and credible sources, I have not and cannot verify absolute accuracy. But then, who can verify data that is thousands of years old?

Table of Contents

Ireland

Trojan

Chapter One

The Journey to Plymouth Rock Begins

Lineage from Adam to where the journey of the two branches of the Soule descendant's we will be following diverge is quite short:

Adam birth is recorded as occurring in Eden 4026 BC and his death 3070 BC. Adam married Eve and they had had eight sons, ten daughters. Adam and Eve lived in the Garden of Eden for more than 129 years when they were banned from Paradise. Adam lived to see the birth of all his descendants except Noah.

Seth Seth Ben Adam, *son of Adam*

Seth ben Adam Second Patriarch married Azura Bint Adam and they had nine sons and seven daughters

Seth was the third son of Adam and Eve mentioned by name in Genesis. Seth was born when Adam was 130 years old. Genesis 5:4 states that Adam fathered "sons and daughters" before his death aged 930 years.

1

Enosh Ben Seth, *son of Seth Ben Adam*

He was born 3765 BC the first son of Seth; born when Seth was 105 years old. He was the Third Patriarch and married Noam, his sister. They had five children together.

At age 90 he begat a son (Cainan): he begat sons and daughters for another 815 years and died at 905 years old. Enosh means "mortal."

Cainan Kenon Ben Enosh *son of Enosh Ben Seth*

Cainan Kenan ben Enos Fourth Patriarch was born and died in Lebanon. He married Mualeleth bint Enos and they had three children together.

He then had two sons and two daughters from another relationship. He died at 910 years of age.

Mahalalel Ben Cainan *son of Cainan Kenon Ben Enosh*

Mahalaleel Ben Cainan has three children with Dinah Barakiel and two more children. He had one brother and one sister.

So all the days of Mahalalel were eight hundred and ninety-five years; and he died. Genesis 5:15-17

2

Jared Ben Mahalaleel, *son of Mahalalel Ben CAINAN*

Jared Ben Mahalaleel had two sons and three daughters. He had seven brothers and one sister. He died in 1422 BC.

Jared was the sixth link in the ten pre-flood generations between Adam and Noah; he lived 962 years (per Genesis 5:18).

Enoch Ben Jared, *son of Jared Ben Mahalaleel –*

Enoch Ben Jared married Edni Bint Daniel in Cainan, East of Eden. They had seven children during their marriage.
He had four brothers and one sister. Enoch Was Taken to Heaven in A chariot of fire, By God. Therebyavoiding the mortal death ascribed to Adam's other descendants.

Methuselah Ben Enoch, *son of Enoch Ben Jared*

Methuselah married Edna Bint Azrail. They had five children during their marriage. He had four brothers.

Methuselah is the oldest man who ever lived. The Bible reports Methuselah was 969

years old when he died.

Methuselah was a descendant of Seth, the third son of Adam and Eve. Methuselah's father was Enoch, his son was Lamech, and his grandson was Noah, who built the ark and rescued the animals from the Great Flood.

Lamech High Priest ben Methuselah, *son of Methuselah Ben Enoch*

Lamech Ninth Patriarch ben Methuselah married Betenos Ashmuh Bat Adah Bat Cainan Barakie and they had 13 children together. He then had one son with Silla Ur. He had six brothers.

From the Writings of Abraham
Lamech, Father of Noah. According to the NOAH was the son of Lamech, the son of Methuselah, the son of Enoch, who was taken up with his city that they might minister unto those in the flesh who sought a higher law than was available to them on the earth.

Now the birth of Noah was after this manner: While his father Lamech was journeying toward his home from preaching the gospel among the sons of men, most of whom had rejected his testimony, an angel of the Lord appeared unto him and saluted him, saying, Hail Lamech, thou favored one of God, for according to the promise of the Lord God to thy father Enoch, thou hast been chosen to be father to him though whom the seed of the Gods will be preserved through the great flood which the Gods will send upon the earth in judgment, for all the sons of men have gone astray through the corruptions of those angels who fell from among the Gods and mingled their seed with the daughters of men and begat sons of great strength and mighty wickedness.

Yea, these have caused all flesh to corrupt their way before the Lord; wherefore they shall be destroyed, save thy son who shall be the seed of the angels.

Noah Ben Lamech, *son of Lamech High Priest ben Methuselah*

Noah's Ark

Noah was the grandson of Methuselah and a tenth generation descendant of Adam, who was the first human being recorded in the Bible.

Scripture tells us Noah was a farmer and was 500 years old when he fathered his three sons: Shem, Ham, and Japheth.

After the Flood, these sons and their wives and their offspring were charged with repopulating the earth.

As an aside, it said that it was from Shem's line that the Messiah, Jesus Christ, as Joseph, earthly father of Jesus Christ is reported to be descended from Methuselah, Shem's great grandfather. Wouldn't it be something if this connection could be made?

Noah's three sons charged with repopulating their world after the flood. The chart below shows how the responsibilities were allocated.

His eldest son, Shem ben Noah's line is the one that the two George Soule branches travel to get to Plymouth Rock.

5

Sons of Noah Disperse to Populate the World

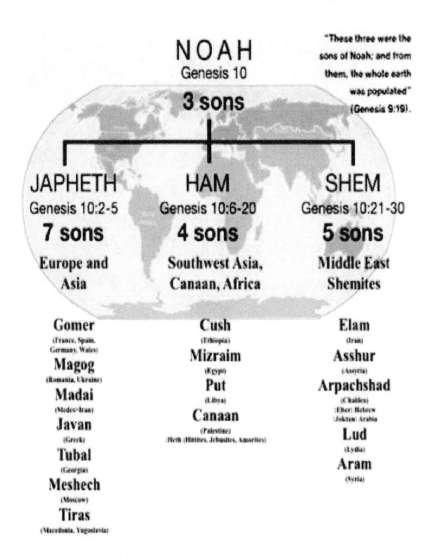

NOAH
Genesis 10

"These three were the sons of Noah; and from them, the whole earth was populated" (Genesis 9:19).

3 sons

JAPHETH
Genesis 10:2-5
7 sons
Europe and Asia

HAM
Genesis 10:6-20
4 sons
Southwest Asia, Canaan, Africa

SHEM
Genesis 10:21-30
5 sons
Middle East Shemites

Gomer
(France, Spain, Germany, Wales)

Magog
(Romania, Ukraine)

Madai
(Medes/Iran)

Javan
(Greek)

Tubal
(Georgia)

Meshech
(Moscow)

Tiras
(Macedonia, Yugoslavia)

Cush
(Ethiopia)

Mizraim
(Egypt)

Put
(Libya)

Canaan
(Palestine)
:Heth (Hittites, Jebusites, Amorites)

Elam
(Iran)

Asshur
(Assyria)

Arpachshad
(Chaldea)
:Eber: Hebrew
:Joktan: Arabia

Lud
(Lydia)

Aram
(Syria)

The Branches Diverge

The first branch follows George "Mayflower" Soule's ancestors journey out of the Garden of Eden to Plymouth Rock following George's wife Mary's lineage.

The second branch follows the line of George and Mary Soules' 3rd great granddaughter Olive. This branch also goes back to Schem ben Noah but travels a completely different course in arriving at Plymouth a few generations after the first line's arrival.

Quick overview of the two Lines

Line #1 – George and Mary Beckett Soule Branch
George and Mary Beckett Soule came to America aboard the Mayflower landing at Plymouth, MA in 1620.

This line began its trip to Plymouth Rock by spreading throughout the Holy Land for a few thousand years and then, around 600BC venture way far away into Ireland! Yes, Ireland. After about 1,400 years ruling Ireland and establishing and ruling Scotland, they ventured across the English Channel to Normandy France about 900 AD to become one with the Norman Knights. They were members of King Arthur's "Knights of the Round Table." So, it was back to back to the Holy land as crusaders.

Then, in 1066 after defeating the English at the Battle of Hastings (Another relative was instrumental in this victory, more later), they returned to England to build forts, castles and live the good life and establish the Great Britain we know today.

Line #2 – Olive Soule Branch

This line follows George "Mayflower" and Mary Soule's 3rd Great Granddaughter, Olive Soule, daughter of Asaph Soule.

The "Olive" branch wanders through the Holy Lands until about 2,200 BC when they find their way into France. They then return to the Holy lands and Asia for a few centuries before travelling into Europe and Germany (Saxony) around the time of the birth of Christ.

From Germany they later made their way back to France settling into and ruling the Normandy Region.

In 1066 the two Soule lines would find themselves together at the Battle of Hastings. After winning the battle they continued to build forts, castles and such and lived happily ever after (well almost for ever after) as the ruling class of England.

Biblical Records and Greek and Roman Mythology
Line #1 follows George and Mary's ancestors journey to Plymouth Rock using the Bible as source of the information for the first part of the trip.

Line #2, the "Olive Branch" information, flows out of the biblical record into Greek and Roman mythology before entering the "modern" era. As a result, don't be surprised if you notice Greek or Norse gods and goddesses in the line of ancestors.

Chapter Two

Mayflower Soule's Begins Their Journey and scatter throughout Asia

Shem ben Noah - *son of Noah Ben Lamech* - **East Eden**

Shem a/k/a "Scaef Sam" was born in Noah's ark and regarded as Noah's eldest son. Genesis 11:10 records that Shem was 100 years old at the birth of his son Arphaxad, two years after the flood; and that he lived for another 500 years after this, making his age at death 600 years.

Asshur prince Son Shem *son of Shem Sceaf* - **Palestine**

Asshur, King of the Assyrian Gods was the second son of Shem. His brothers were Elam, Arphaxad, Lud, and Aram. Asshur is considered the father of Assyrians. He gave power and life to every priestly king.

A winged circle or globe with the human figure of a warrior god armed with a bow in its center was used to symbolize him as "the great god, king of all gods." Also, Asshur was used as part of a compound name for various Assyrian kings that followed.

The text of Genesis 10:11 is somewhat ambiguous as to whether it was Asshur himself, or Nimrod who, according to Biblical tradition, built the Assyrian cities of Nineveh, Resen, Rehoboth-Ir and Calah, since the name *Asshur* can refer to both the person and the country. Sir Walter Raleigh devoted several pages in his *History of the World* to reciting theories regarding the question of whether it had been Nimrod or Asshur who built the cities in Assyria

Decendant *of and only son of Asshur prince Son Shem –* Phoenicia

Nothing much has been noted about Asshur's only son (including his name) except that he was the father of Elhbaal DeTyre, King of Israel and grandfather of the famous Queen Jezebel

Elhbaal DeTyre, King od Israel - *son of Asshur Descendants –* Phoenicia

Ethobaal I was the king of Tyre who founded a new dynasty. During his reign, Tyre expanded its power on the mainland, making all of Phoenicia its territory as far north as Beirut, including Sidon, and even a part of the island of Cyprus. At the same time, Tyre also built new overseas colonies: Botrys (now Batrun) near Byblos, and Auza in Libya. Primary information related to Ithobaal comes from Josephus's citation of the Phoenician author Menander of Ephesus, in *Against Apion* i.18. Here it is said that the previous king, Phelles, "was slain by

Ithobalus, the priest of Astarte, who reigned thirty-two years, and lived sixty-eight years; he was succeeded by his son Badezorus (Baal-Eser II)."

The dates given here are according to the work of F. M. Cross and others who take 825 BC as the date of Dido's flight from her brother Pygmalion, after which she founded the city of Carthage in 814 BC.

Ethobaal held close diplomatic contacts with king Ahab of Israel. First Kings 16:31 relates that his daughter Jezebel married Ahab (874 – 853 BC), and Phoenician influence in Samaria and the other Israelite cities was extensive. In the 1 Kings passage, Ethobaal is

Ethobaal's famous daughter Jezebel

labeled king of the Sidonians. At this time Tyre and Sidon were consolidated into one kingdom.

Menander's comment that Ethobaal had been a priest of Astarte before becoming king explains why his daughter Jezebel was so zealous in the promotion of the Phoenician gods, thus leading to the conflicts between Elijah and Jezebel's forces described in 1 Kings 18 and 19. Menander's further statement that her father was a murderer sheds some light on her choice of a way to solve the "Naboth" problem in 1 Kings 21.

Jezebel deTyre - *daughter of Elhbaal DeTyre, King of Israel –*
Phoenicia

According to the Hebrew Bible, Jezebel incited her husband King
Ahab to abandon the worship of Yahweh and encourage worship

of the deities Baal and
Asherah instead.
Jezebel persecuted the
prophets of Yahweh,
and fabricated
evidence of blasphemy
against an innocent
landowner who
refused to sell his
property to King Ahab, causing the landowner to be put to death.

As a result of these transgressions against God and people of
Israel, Jezebel met a gruesome death. Members of her own court
retinue threw her out of a window. When they went to bury her,
they found no more of her than her skull, feet and the palms of her
hands.

When King Jehu was told of this he said, "This is the word of the
Lord, which he spoke by his servant
Elijah the Tishbite: '*In the territory of
Jezreel the dogs shall eat the flesh of
Jezebel, and the corpse of Jezebel
shall be as dung on the face of the
field in the territory of Jezreel, so that
no one can say, This is Jezebel.*'" -
2Kings 9:35-37

Jezebel became associated with false
prophets. In some interpretations, her
dressing in finery and putting on
makeup led to the association of the
use of cosmetics with "painted
women" or prostitutes.

*Jezebel being thrown
from a window*

Ahab ben Omri 10th King of Israel - *son of Jezebel deTyre –* **Israel**

Ahab became king of Israel in the thirty-eighth year of Asa, king of Judah, and reigned for twenty-two years. William F. Albright dated his reign to 869–850 BC, while E. R. Thiele offered the dates 874–853 BC. Michael D. Coogan dates his reign to 871–852 BC. Omri (Ahab's father and founder of the short-lived Omri Dynasty) seems to have been a successful military leader; he is reported in the text of the Moabite Mesha Stele to have "oppressed Moab for many days". During Ahab's reign, Moab, which had been conquered by his father, remained tributary. Ahab was allied by marriage with Jehoshaphat, who was king of Judah. Only with Aram Damascus is he believed to have had strained relations.

Jecolia Jecoliah Yecholiah Jerusalem - *daughter of Ahab ben Omri 10th* **Israel**

Queen Jecolia Jecoliah Yecholiah Jerusalem was born in 868 BC at Jerusalem, Israel, and died in Israel. She had eight sons and one daughter.

Uzziah Azzariah Azariah ben Amaziah, 12th King of JUDAH (826 - 758) *son of Jecolia Jecoliah Yecholiah Jerusalem* - **Judah, Iraq**

Uzziah took the throne at the age of 16, and reigned for about 52 years. His reign was "the most prosperous excepting that of

Jehoshaphat since the time of Solomon."

In the earlier part of his reign, under the influence of a prophet named Zechariah, he was faithful to God, and "did that which was right in the sight of the Lord" (2 Kings 15:3; 2 Chronicles 26:4-5)

In Jerusalem he made machines designed by skillful men for use on the towers and on the corner defenses to shoot arrows and hurl large stones. According to 2 Chron. 26, Uzziah conquered the Philistines and the Arabians, and received tribute from the Ammonites. He refortified the country, reorganized and reequipped the army, and personally engaged in agricultural pursuits. He was a vigorous and able ruler, and "his name spread abroad, even to the entering in of Egypt". (2 Chronicles 26:8-14)

Then his pride led to his downfall. He entered the temple of the Lord to burn incense on the altar of incense. Azariah the High Priest saw this as an attempt to usurp the prerogatives of the priests and confronted him with a band of eighty priests, saying, "It is not right for you, Uzziah, to burn incense to the LORD. That is for the priests, the descendants of Aaron, who have been consecrated to burn incense." (2 Chronicles 26:18) In the meantime a great earthquake shook the ground and a rent was made in the temple, and the bright rays of the sun shone through it, and fell upon the king's face, insomuch that the leprosy seized upon him immediately. (Josephus Flavius, Antiquities IX 10:4). Uzziah was suddenly struck with *tzaraat* while in the act of offering incense (2 Chronicles 26:19-21), and he was driven from the Temple and compelled to reside in "a separate house" until his death (2 Kings 15:5, 27; 2 Chronicles 26:3).

The government was turned over to his son Jotham (2 Kings 15:5), a co-regency that lasted for the last 11 years of Uzziah's life (751/750 to 740/739 BC).

He was buried in a separate grave "in the field of the burial which belonged to the kings" (2 Kings 15:7; 2 Chr. 26:23). "That lonely grave in the royal necropolis would eloquently testify to coming generations that all earthly monarchy must bow before the inviolable order of the divine will, and that no interference could be tolerated with that unfolding of the purposes of God... (Dr. Green's *Kingdom of Israel*).

Ahaz ben Jotham King Of Judah, And The Bloodline of Joseph - *son of Uzziah Azzariah Azariah ben Amaziah, 12th King of ben Amaziah, 12th King of JUDAH* - **Palestine, Israel**

Ahaz's reign commenced at the age of 20, in the 17th year of the reign of Pekah of Israel. It is described in 2 Kings 16; Isaiah 7-9;

Destruction of Northern Kingdom|
Immediately upon his accession Ahaz had to meet a coalition formed by northern Israel, under Pekah, and Damascus (Syria), under Rezin. These kings wished to compel him to join them in opposing the Assyrians, who were arming a force against the Northern Kingdom under Tiglath-Pileser III. (Pul). To protect himself Ahaz called in the aid of the Assyrians. Tiglath-Pileser sacked Damascus and annexed Aram. According to 2 Kings 16:9, the population of Aram was deported and Rezin executed. Tiglath-Pileser then attacked Israel and "took Ijon, Abel Beth Maacah, Janoah, Kedesh and Hazor. He took Gilead and Galilee, including all the land of Naphtali, and deported the people to Assyria." Tiglath-Pileser also records this act in one of his inscriptions.

Through Assyria's intervention, and as a result of its invasion and subjection of the kingdom of Damascus and the Kingdom of Israel, Ahaz was relieved of his troublesome neighbors; but his protector henceforth claimed and held suzerainty over his kingdom. This war of invasion lasted two years (734-732 BC), and ended in the capture and annexation of Damascus to Assyria and of the territory of Israel north of the border of Jezreel. Ahaz in the meanwhile furnished auxiliaries to Tiglath-Pileser. This appeal to Assyria met with stern opposition from the prophet Isaiah, who counseled Ahaz to rely upon the Lord and not upon outside aid. The sequel seemed to justify the king and to condemn the prophet. Ahaz, during his whole reign, was free from troubles[1] with which the neighboring rulers were harassed, who from time to time revolted against Assyria. Thus it was that, in 722, Samaria was taken and northern Israel wholly incorporated into the Assyrian empire.

Religious observance]

Ahaz, who was irresolute and impressionable, yielded readily to the glamour and prestige of the Assyrians in religion as well as in politics. In 732 he went to Damascus to swear homage to Tiglath-Pileser and his gods; and, taking a fancy to an altar, which he saw there, he had one like it made in Jerusalem, which, with a corresponding change in ritual, he made a permanent feature of the Temple worship. Changes were also made in the arrangements and furniture of the Temple, "because of the king of Assyria" (II Kings, xvi. 18). Furthermore, Ahaz fitted up an astrological observatory with accompanying sacrifices, after the fashion of the ruling people. In other ways Ahaz lowered the character of the national worship. It is recorded that he even offered his son by fire to Moloch.

His government is considered by the Deuteronomistic historian, as having been disastrous to the religious state of the country; and a large part of the reforming work of his son Hezekiah was aimed at undoing the evil that Ahaz had done.

Succession

He died at the age of 36 and was succeeded by his son, Hezekiah. Because of his wickedness he was "not brought into the sepulchre of the kings" (2 Chronicles 28:27). An insight into Ahaz's neglect of the worship of the Lord is found in the statement that on the first day of the month of Nisan that followed Ahaz's death, his son Hezekiah commissioned the priests and Levites to open and repair the doors of the Temple and to remove the defilements of the sanctuary, a task which took 16 days. (2 Chronicles 29:3-20)

Hezekiah ben Ahaz King of Judah - *son of Ahaz ben Jotham King Of Judah, And The Bloodline of Joseph* **Jerusalem, Judah, Palestine, Israel**

Archaeologist Edwin Thiele has concluded that his reign was between c. 715 and 686 BC. He is also one of the most prominent kings of Judah mentioned in the Hebrew Bible and is one of the kings mentioned in the **genealogy of Jesus** in the Gospel of Matthew.

According to the Hebrew Bible, Hezekiah witnessed the destruction of the northern Kingdom of Israel by Sargon's Assyrians in c. 720 BC and was king of Judah during the invasion and siege of Jerusalem by Sennacherib in 701 BC. Hezekiah enacted sweeping religious reforms, including a strict mandate for the sole worship of Yahweh and a prohibition on venerating other deities within the Temple in Jerusalem. Isaiah and Micah prophesied during his reign.

According to the Hebrew Bible, Hezekiah assumed the throne of Judah at the age of 25 and reigned for 29 years (2 Kings 18:2). Some writers have proposed that Hezekiah served as coregent with his father Ahaz for about 14 years. His sole reign is dated by William F. Albright as 715–687 BC, and by Edwin R. Thiele as 716–687 BC (the last ten years being a co-regency with his son Manasseh).

Hezekiah purified and repaired the Temple, purged its idols, and reformed the priesthood. In an effort to abolish what he considered idolatry from his kingdom, he destroyed the high places (or bamot) and "bronze serpent" (or "Nehushtan"), recorded as being made by Moses, which became objects of idolatrous worship. In place of this, he centralized the worship of

God at the Jerusalem Temple. Hezekiah also resumed the Passover pilgrimage and the tradition of inviting the scattered tribes of Israel to take part in a Passover festival. He sent messengers to Ephraim and Manasseh inviting them to Jerusalem for the celebration of the Passover.

The messengers, however, were not only not listened to, but were even laughed at; only a few men of Asher, Manasseh, and Zebulun came to Jerusalem. Nevertheless, the Passover was celebrated with great solemnity and such rejoicing as had not been in Jerusalem since the days of Solomon. Hezekiah is portrayed by the Hebrew Bible as a great and good king.

Menasseh ben Hezekiah King Of Judah -*son of Hezekiah ben*

Ahaz King Of Judah - Jerusalem, Judah, Palestine, Israel Menasseh was the only son of Hezekiah with Hephzibah. He became king at an age of 12 and reigned for 55 years (2 Kings 21:1; 2 Chronicles 33:1). He began his reign as co-regent with his father Hezekiah. Manasseh was the first king of Judah who would not have had a direct experience with the Kingdom of Israel (Samaria), which had been destroyed by the Assyrians and reversed the religious changes made by his father Hezekiah.

He married Meshullemeth, daughter of Haruz of Jotbah, and they had a son Amon, who succeeded him as king of Judah. When he died he was buried in the garden of Uzza, the "garden of his own house" (2 Kings 21:17–18; 2 Chronicles 33:20), and not in the City of David, among his ancestors. The biblical account of Manasseh is found in II Kings 21:1–18 and II Chronicles 32:33–33:20. He is also mentioned in Jeremiah 15:4.

Amon Assur ben Judah Judah -*son of Judah Menasseh ben Hezekiah King Of Judah* - Palestine, Israel

Amon was the son of King Manasseh of Judah and Meshullemeth,

 a daughter of Haruz of Jotbah. Although the date is unknown, the Hebrew Bible records that he married Jedidah, the daughter of Adaiah of Bozkath. Amon began his reign of Judah at the age of 22, and reigned for two years.

The Hebrew Bible records that Amon continued his father Manasseh's practice of idolatry and set up pagan images as his father had done. II Kings states that Amon "did that which was evil in the sight of YAWEH, as did Manasseh his father. And he walked in all the way that his father walked in, and served the idols that his father served, and worshipped them." Similarly, II Chronicles records that "...he did that which was evil in the sight of the Lord, as did Manasseh his father; and Amon sacrificed unto all the graven images which Manasseh his father had made, and served them." The Talmudic tradition recounts that "Amon burnt the Torah, and allowed spider webs to cover the altar [through complete disuse] ... Amon sinned very much." Like other textual sources, Flavius Josephus too criticizes the reign of Amon, describing his reign similarly to the Bible.

After reigning two years, Amon was assassinated by his servants, who conspired against him, and was succeeded by his son Josiah, who at the time was eight years old. After Amon's assassination his murderers became unpopular with the people, and were ultimately killed. Some scholars assert that Amon was assassinated because people disliked the heavy influence that Assyria, an age-old enemy of Judah responsible for the destruction of the Kingdom of Israel, had upon him.

19

Josiah ben Amon King Of Judah - *son of Amon Assur ben Judah Judah* - **Jerusalem**

According to the Bible, Josiah was the son of King Amon and Jedidah, the daughter of Adaiah of Bozkath. His grandfather Manasseh was one of the kings blamed for turning away from the worship of Yahweh. Manasseh adapted the Temple for idolatrous worship. Josiah's great-grandfather was King Hezekiah who was a noted reformer.

Josiah had four sons: Johanan, and Eliakim by Zebudah the daughter of Pedaiah of Rumah; (Eliakim had his name changed by Pharaoh Necho of Egypt to Jehoiakim 2 Kings 23:34) and Mattanyahu and Shallum both by Hamutal, the daughter of Libnah.

Shallum succeeded Josiah as king of Judah, under the name Jehoahaz. Shallum was succeeded by Eliakim, under the name Jehoiakim, who was succeeded by his own son Jeconiah; then Jeconiah was succeeded to the throne by Mattanyahu, under the name Zedekiah. Zedekiah was the last king of Judah before the kingdom was conquered by Babylon and the people exiled.

Zedekiah / Mattaniah ben Josiah "The Last King Of Judah"
King Of Judah *son of Josiah ben Amon King Of Judah -*
Jerusalem

Last King of Judah - According to the Hebrew Bible, Zedekiah

was made king of Judah by Nebuchadnezzar II in 597 BCE at the age of twenty-one. This is in agreement with a Babylonian records, which state, The *seventh year: In the month Kislev the king of Akkad mustered his army and marched to Hattu. He encamped against the city of Judah and on the second day of the month Adar he captured the city (and) seized (its) king. A king of his own choice he appointed in the city (and) taking the vast tribute he brought it into Babylon.*

Despite the strong formal protest of Jeremiah, Baruch ben Neriah and his other family and advisors, as well as the example of Jehoiakim, he revolted against Babylon, and entered into an alliance with Pharaoh Hophra of Egypt. Nebuchadnezzar responded by invading Judah. Nebuchadnezzar began a siege of Jerusalem in December 589 BC. During this siege, which lasted about thirty months, "every worst woe befell the city, which drank the cup of God's fury to the dregs".)

At the end of his eleven-year reign, Nebuchadnezzar succeeded in capturing Jerusalem. Zedekiah and his followers attempted to escape, making their way out of the city, but were captured on the plains of Jericho, and were taken to Riblah.

Zedekiah, who was descended from the royal line of David and all of his sons were captured and taken from Jerusalem to Babylon, where his sons were slain in front of Zedekiah's eyes and then he was blinded, so that the execution of his sons would be the last thing he ever saw. He himself died in prison, in Babylon, and all of this was because he betrayed God and his people i.e.: broke

21

The Covenant and caused his people to suffer poverty under his own laws, instead of prosperity under God's Laws in The Covenant that is written in The Torah

Go Ye to "the Isles" Which Lay to the North and West of Judea

Destruction of Jerusalem

In the book of Jeremiah we read how Ishmael liberated a number of the captives, including the prophet Jeremiah and *'the kings daughters'*. Jeremiah was instructed by God to go to the lands, which lay to the north and west of Judea; his destination was to be *'the Isles'*, which have traditionally been identified with the British Isles, including Eire or Ireland. After the fall of Jerusalem, Nebuzaradan was sent to destroy it. The city was plundered and razed to the ground. Solomon's Temple was destroyed. Only a small number of vineyard workers and farmers were permitted to remain in the land.

Chapter Three

Biblical Ancestors Venture into Ireland before 600BC

Tamar Tea Thephi ben Zedikiah "Daughter Of God's
House" **Queen Of Ireland / Princess Of Judah And Of The
House Of David** *daughter of Zedekiah / Mattaniah ben Josiah
"The Last King Of Judah" King Of Judah -* **Judah**

Exedous from Jerusalem

Teia Tephi became the queen of Ireland on the 21st of June in 583
B.C, the queen, who came to Ireland from Jerusalem. She was
descended from the Jacob who had his name changed by God to
Israel at Bethel (God's Place). Here is where he set up a stone
pillar to use as a pillow, as is recorded in the Book of Genesis.
During the destruction of Jerusalem, by King Nebuchadnezzar in
588 B.C., the biblical Jeremiah hid with Tamar Tea, Zedekiah's
daughter under the Temple, built by Solomon, in a cave where
The Ark of The Covenant was hidden along with *Jacob's Pillar
(The Bethel/ Lia Fail Stone)* which is king David's Throne of
Israel.

The Story of the The Bethel/Lia Fail Stone/the Coronation Stone

Jacob dreaming with his head on the Stone

The Stone is a block of hand-cut red sandstone, supposed to have originated near the Dead Sea, and upon which Jacob, who later became known as Israel, rested his head on the evening that he had a vision of angels ascending and descending the ladder to Heaven. The High Kings, of Eire and Ireland were crowned while standing upon the Stone.

The stone sat in Westminster Abbey, England, is the coronation stone of the Hebrew nation called Israelites. The stone was named Beth-el (house of God) by the patriarch Israel (sometimes called Jacob) roughly 2000 BC and remained with his descendents. It travelled with them for forty years in the wilderness, supplying their water, and was preserved and brought to Ireland in 583 BC by the prophet Jeremiah; eventually

The Coronation Stone/The Bethel/Lia Fail Stone

being transferred to Scotland, then England, and now resides in Scotland.

Notice the groove worn deeply into the Rock between the two metal rings. This would have to result from many years of carrying the Rock on a pole. And this had to have happened before 583 BC when Jeremiah brought the Rock to Ireland, because it has been moved a very few miles in the last 2500 years. This groove is the result of being carried around the wilderness for forty years. Irish legend says that any imposter or unrightful heir to the throne would be known by the fact that the stone would roar ONLY when the rightful king stood on it.

Hill of Tara, Myth and Legend

The Annals of The Kingdom of Ireland note:
"Tea, daughter of Lughaidh, son of Ith, whom Eremhon married in Spain, to the repudiation of Odhbha, was the Tea who requested of Eremhon a choice hill, as her dower, in whatever place she should select it, that she might be interred therein, and that her mound and her gravestone might be thereon raised, and where every prince ever to be born of her race should dwell. The guarantees who undertook to execute this for her were Amhergin Gluingeal and Emhear Finn. The hill she selected was Druim Caein, i.e. Teamhair. It is from her it was called, and in it was she interred."

The hill, which was named for Tea / Tamar Tephi is still known by the name of *Tara*, and is honored as the traditional seat of the High Kings of Eire. It is claimed that with the Princess Tea Tephi,

Aerial view of The Hill of Tara

were brought to Ireland many priceless relics showing the Hebrew identity, and royal descent of her people; among them the "Jodham Morain" or priest breast plate; the harp of King David, "Sweet Singer of Israel", and the famous Coronation Stone of the Kings of Ireland, Scotland, and England.

An Ancient Love Story

Tamar Tea arrived with the <u>Bethel / Lia Fail Stone</u> and her two handmaidens, at Pen Edair (Binn Eadair - Howth), near Ath Cliath (Dublin), in Ireland on the 18th of June 583 B.C. She was greeted there by Eochaidh, the High king (Ard ri - Heremon) and Ethan, the king's harper and good friend, between whom she was carried ashore. Both instantly fell in love with the queen.

Teia Tephi knew only the identity of the harper (Ethan) and didn't know that the other person carrying her was actually Eochaidh, the High-king, whom she was destined to marry. She stayed that night at the Fort of Crimthann, which was built on the top of Howth Hill.

Eochaidh, who was urgently called away to rescue his sister who had been kidnapped, had, as a child, been given a vision and told that he must not marry, even if he reached middle-age, because one day his queen would come from the East. When he received the message from Elatha, that the queen was coming from Jerusalem to live in Ireland, he realized that his wait was almost over and his boyhood prophetical-vision was about to become reality.

Teia Tephi was then escorted to Cathair Crofinn (The Hill of Tara), where she arrived on the 20th of June in 583 B.C. and was escorted to the house that had already been prepared for her (Rath Grainne - Fort of the Seed) there, over the door of which the Druids had written *'Jerusalem'*, in Hebrew.

Pagan Symbol Banished

At Tara, there were a number of priests of the satanic Baal-religion who had erected a phallic-pillarstone as part of their worship of the mythical gods of pagan Baal fertility. Teia Tephi had brought with her The Torah or God's Laws, which state that worshipping false gods and making graven images of these, or anything else, is strictly prohibited and carries the death penalty (The Second Commandment), so she ordered that the obscene stone phallus be removed immediately and the Stone of Destiny/Bethel Stone / Lia Fail be put in its place on the Forrad (Inauguration Mound).

Baal-priests and they removed the phallic Baal-pillar from the Inauguration Mound (Forrad) and buried it near where Duma na nGiall (Teamur - Tephi's wall -

The Mound of the Hostages not far from The Stone of Destiny

now known as The Mound of The Hostages) stands today.

The Hill of Tara, was once the ancient seat of power in Ireland – 142 kings are said to have reigned there in prehistoric and historic times. In ancient Irish religion and mythology Temair was the sacred place of dwelling for the gods, and was the entrance to the otherworld.

Saint Patrick is said to have come to Tara to confront the ancient religion of the pagans at its most powerful site

At the Hill of Tara, Irish myth, legend and history are one - this magical site has been home to gods and goddesses, to druids and warriors, and to Ireland's High Kings. Tara is imbued with a magical, mythical atmosphere. It is the stuff of legends, the home of gods and heroes, not mere mortals.

The Hill of Tara has a strange effect on people. From up here on the heights one sees not only into the distance, but into Tara's past. Tara has more than its share of heady stories to tell - tales of intoxicating drinks, chariot-driving High Kings and old hags who transformed themselves into beautiful women.

Listen out for the Lia Fail (The stone of destiny) - singing stones

The "Stone of Destiny" atop Hill of Tara

which announce the presence of future kings. The past is visibly engraved in the undulating landscape at Tara where the hillside is marked by ancient earthworks, mound formations and the ruins of royal enclosures.

The Hill of Tara is reputed to allow a glimpse of no less than 25% of the Irish mainland. On a clear day you will believe this. That is, if you can brave the ups and downs of the quite rough landscape. There are no proper paths and visitors will sometimes have to scramble through the ditches at the mercy of slippery grass and sheep droppings.

The reward of your troubles will be a close encounter with ceremonial enclosures, passage tombs and landscaped areas with no apparent (or at least obvious) reason for their existence. Indeed the whole area is so steeped in mystery that it was partly destroyed around a hundred years ago ...by the "British Israelites" searching for the Ark of the Covenant.

The Biblical Story of the Coronation Stone

*Genesis 28:11 And he (Jacob) lighted upon a certain place, and tarried there all night, because the sun was set; and he took of the **stones** of that place, and put [them for] his pillows, and lay down in that place to sleep.*
28:12 And he dreamed, and behold a ladder set up on the earth, and the top of it reached to heaven: and behold the angels of God ascending and descending on it.
28:13 And, behold, the "I AM" stood above it, and said, I [am] the "I AM" God of Abraham thy father, and the God of Isaac: the land whereon thou liest, to thee will I give it, and to thy seed;

28

28:14 And thy seed (Jacob's) shall be as "the dust of the earth", and thou shalt spread abroad to the West (U.S.A.?), and to the East (Australia?), and to the North (Canada?), and to the South (Africa?): and in thee and in thy seed shall all the families of the earth be blessed.

King David praising God
singing and playing the harp

28:15 And, behold, I [am] with thee, and will keep thee in all [places] where thou goest, and will bring thee again into this land; for I will not leave thee, until I have done [that] which I have spoken to thee of.

28:16 And Jacob awaked out of his sleep, and he said, Surely the "I AM" is in this place; and I knew [it] not.

28:17 And he was afraid, and said, How dreadful [is] this place! this [is] none other but the house of God, and this [is] the gate of heaven.

*28:18 And Jacob rose up early in the morning, and took **the Stone** that he had put [for] his pillows, and set it up [for] a **pillar**, and poured oil upon the top of it.*

*28:19 And he called the name of that place Bethel (House of God): but the name of that city [was called] **Luz** at the first.*

28:20 And Jacob vowed a vow, saying, If God will be with me, and will keep me in this way that I go, and will give me bread to eat, and clothing to put on,

28:21 So that I come again to my father's house in peace; then shall the "I AM" be my God:

*28:22 And **this Stone**, which I have set [for] a **pillar**, shall be God's house (Bethel): and of all that Thou shalt give me I will surely give the tenth unto Thee.*

Out of Biblical Records,
Into Irish History

Ancient Tara Castle

Condla Cáem Ard-rí na h'Éireann Conla Caomh Mac h-Eirora Uí Éremóin *son of Tamar Tea Thephi ben Zedikiah "Daughter Of God's House" Queen Of Ireland / Princess Of Judah And Of The House Of David -* **Tara Castle, Meath, Leinster, Ireland**

Condla Cáem Ard-rí na h'Éireann Conla Caomh Mac h-Eirora Uí Éremóin had one son with Muirion nic Fiachadh Ariade.
He then married Sabhdh Ingen Logha and they had three children together. He had one brother. He lived from 491 BC to – 442 BC

Ailtleathan *son of Condla Cáem Ard-rí na h'Éireann Conla Caomh Mac h-Eirora Uí Éremóin -* **Tara, Ireland**

King Eochaidh "The Long Haired" Ailtleathan – King of All Ireland (460 - 418) married Agnus of Ireland. They had three children during their marriage. He had two brothers.

Year 460 BC was a year of the pre-Julian Roman calendar. At the time, it was known as the Year of the Consulship of Poplicola and Sabinus. The year 460 BC has been used since the early medieval period, when the Anno Domini calendar era became the prevalent method in Europe for naming years.

Aengus Tuirmeach *son of Eochaidh (King) "The Long Haired" Ailtleathan –* **Scotland**

Aengus Tuirmeach had two sons and one daughter with Magach Ingen Fergusa. He was the 81st High King of Ireland. He was brother of Conall Collamrach mac Echdach, Rí na h'Éireann.

Aengus Tuirmeach was ancestor of the Kings of Dalriada, and Argyle in Scotland. Aenghus slew Fearghus Fortamhail to become the eighty-first monarch of Ireland ca. 384 BC and reigned for thirty years before being killed in a battle at Tara in BC 324

Eanda Aighnach *son of Aengus Tuirmeach* - **Tara, Ireland**

Eanda Aighnach 'the Hospitable,' 84th High King Enna slew Nia Sedhamain to become king ca. 312 BC and reigned for twenty eight years. He had one son with his wife Enna Aighneach.

He was slain at the battle of Ard-Crimhthainn by Crimhthann Cosgrah.

King Labhra Luire *son of Eanda Aighnach* - **Ireland**

Labhra of Ireland Luirc "The Fierce," probably was an unwelcome change after his father "The Hospitable". He had one child with Labhra Luire Ireland, a son, Blathachta "of Ireland". He died in 100 BC

Blathladhta Prince Eamhna (- 100) *son of Labhra Luire -*
Dublin, Leinster, Ireland

Blathladhta EAMHNA, Prince of
Ireland (son of *Labhra LUIRE, Prince
of Ireland*) died 100 BC. He had two
sons including Easamhuin EAMHNA,
Prince of Ireland,

Easamhuin Eamhna *son of Blathladhta Prince Eamhna -*
Dublin, Leinster, Dublin, Ireland Essamain Emna
MacBLATHACHTA (Prince) of IRELAND   Easamhuin)

Eamhna (Eamnadh) was born in 60 in Dublin, Ireland.
He had three sons with Magach (Princess) of IRELAND. He died
in 100 in Dublin, Ireland, at the age of 40.
He was excluded from the Throne by his father's murderer.

He was King George I's 50th-Great Grandfather.

Roignen "the Red" Ruadh Prince of Ireland *son of Easamhuin Eamhna* - **Dublin, Leinster, Dublin, Ireland**

Roignen `the Red' Ruadh Prince of IRELAND, son of Essamain Emna MacBLATHACHTA Prince of IRELAND. He married Magach Princess of IRELAND and had one child, Fionnlogh (Finnlaoch) Prince in IRELAND.

During his reign the cattle in Ireland were nearly all wiped out because of a disease called Murrain. It is a highly infectious disease of cattle and sheep and literally means "death." The population of that era had no way of identifying specific diseases in their livestock so they simply put all illnesses under one heading. There were major sheep and cattle murrains in Europe during the 14th century, which when combined with the Little Ice Age, resulted in widespread famine during the Great Famine.

Finligha of Ireland *son of Roignen Ruadh* - **Dublin, Leinster, Dublin, Ireland**

Fionnlogh Son Roighneim, 90th High King of Ireland, was born in 187. Fionnlogh married Benla Daughter of Creombthan of Ireland. Benla was born in Dublin, Leinster, Ireland. They had one son: Fionn Macfionnloch OHenna 92nd High King of Ireland and one other child. Finligha died in 210

Fionn Macfionnloch O Henna *son of Finligha Of Ireland* - **Tara, Ireland**

Fionn Macfionnloch O Henna was born in 172. He married Benta Benia, daughter of Criomthan. They had seven children during their marriage.

Eochaidh Feidhlioch *son of Fionn Macfionnloch O Henna* - **Tara,**

Eochaidh Feidhlioch 93rd King of Ireland married CLOTHFIONN UCHTLEATHAN. They had 13 children during their marriage. He had five brothers and one sister. He was born in 180 BC and died 130 BC

By him Clothfionn, daughter of Eochaidh Uchtleathan had triplets - Breas, Nar, and Lothar (the Fineamhas), who were slain at the battle of Dromchriadh; after their death, a melancholy settled on the Monarch, hence his name "Feidhlioch."

This Monarch caused the division of the Kingdom by Ugaine Mór into twenty-five parts, to cease; and ordered that the ancient  Firvolgian division into Provinces should be resumed, viz., Two Munsters, Leinster, Conacht, and Ulster.

He also divided the government of these Provinces amongst his favourite courtiers: - Conacht he divided into three parts between Fiodhach, Eochaidh Allat, and Tinne, son of Conragh, son of Ruadhri Mór, No 62 on the "Line of Ir;" Ulster (Uladh) he gave to Feargus, the son of Leighe; Leinster he gave to Ros, the son of Feargus Fairge; and the two Munsters he gave to Tighernach Teadhbheamach and Deagbadah.

After this division of the Kingdom, Eochaidh proceeded to erect a Royal Palace in Conacht; this he built on Tinne's government in a place called Druin-na-n Druagh, now Craughan (from Craughan Crodhearg, Maedhbh's mother, to whom she gave the palace), but previously, Rath Eochaidh. About the same time he bestowed his daughter the Princess Maedhbh on Tinne, whom he constituted King of Conacht; Maedhbh being hereditary Queen of that Province.

After many years reign Tinne was slain by Maceacht (or Monaire) at Tara. After ten years' undivided reign, Queen Maedhbh married Oilioll Mór, son of Ros Ruadh, of Leinster, to whom she bore the seven Maine; Oilioll Mór was slain by Conall Cearnach, who was soon after killed by the people of Conacht. Maedhbh was slain by Ferbhuidhe, the son of Conor MacNeasa (Neasa was his mother); but in reality this Conor was the son of Fachtna Fathach, son of Cas, son of Ruadhri Mór, of the Line of Ir.

Cloth FIONN *daughter of EOCHAIDH FEIDHLIOCH* - **Tara, Offaly, Ireland**

Cloth FIONN had four daughters with Fargall King of DENMARK.

She then married Eochaidh Feidhlioch Ireland and they had 12 children together. She had seven brothers and five sisters. She died in Tara, Offaly, Ireland.

Dervorgill Ireland Denmark *daughter of Cloth FIONN* – **Dublin**

Dervorgill Ireland Denmark was born in 34 AD in Denmark. She married King Alba and they had six children together.

She then married Lugaidh Sriabhn 98th Monarch Dearg High King of Ireland and they had four children together.

Eithne of Alba *daughter of Dervorgill Ireland Denmark -* **Dublin,**

When Eithne of Alba was born in 113 in Coni, Piemonte, Italy, her father, King Alba (Scotland), was 25 and her mother, Dervorgill, was 19. She had three sons and one daughter. She died in 194 having lived 81 years.

Eithne, daughter of the king of Alba, wife of the High King Fiacha Finnfolaidh and mother of Tuathal Teachtmhar

Her Husband Fiacha, was, according to medieval Irish legend and historical tradition, a High King of Ireland. He, and the freemen of Ireland, were killed in an uprising of *aithech-tuatha* or "subject peoples." His wife Eithne, daughter of the king of Alba (Scotland), who was pregnant, fled home to Alba, where she gave birth to Fiacha son, Tuathal Techtmar, who would ultimately return to Ireland to claim the throne

Fafertach Princess of Ireland *daughter of King Eithne Of Alba -* **Dublin, Leinster, Ireland**Fafertach

Princess of Ireland had two sons with Mug Corb Maghcorb MacConchobuir Abratruaid Prince of Ireland between 179 and 198.

Dublin

Fer Cob MacMoga Monarch Ireland (198 -) *son of Fafertach Princess of Ireland* - **Thomond, Ireland**

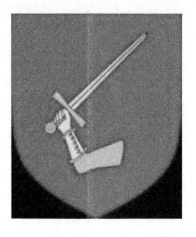

When Fer Cob MacMoga Monarch Ireland was born in 198 his mother, Fafertach, was 44. He had one son and one brother.

He ruled Thomond, a kingdom of Gaelic Ireland, associated geographically with present-day County Clare and County Limerick, as well as parts of County Tipperary.
The kingdom existed from the collapse of the Kingdom of Munster as competition between the Ó Briain and the Mac Cárthaigh led to the schism between Thomond (North Munster) and Desmond (South Munster). It continued to exist outside of the Anglo-Norman controlled Lordship of Ireland until the 16th century.

Amadair Flidais Foltchain MacFer, 78th Monarch of Ireland *son of Fer Cob MacMoga Monarch Ireland* – **Ireland**

Adamair (Adammair, Adhamair, Amadir), son of Fer Corb, was, according to medieval Irish legends and historical traditions, a High King of Ireland. He came from Munster, killed the previous incumbent, Ailill Caisfhiaclach, and reigned for five years, until he was killed by Eochaid Ailtleathan. He was the husband of the presumed goddess Flidais of the Tuatha Dé Danann

King Nia Segaman MacAmadair Monarch of Ireland *son of Amadair Flidais Foltchain MacFer, 78th Monarch of Ireland* - **Ireland**

Nia Segamain, was, according to medieval Irish legend and historical tradition, a High King of Ireland. His mother is presumed to be the woodland goddess Flidais of the Tuatha Dé Danann, whose magic made wild does give milk as freely as domesticated cattle during his reign.

He ruled for seven years, until he was killed by Énna Aignech. His name means "sister's son or champion of Segamon", and is perhaps related to Segomo, an ancient Gaulish deity equated in Roman times with Mars and Hercules. A slightly more historical Nia Segamain occurs in early Eóganachta pedigrees, and this is sometimes interpreted as evidence for the Gaulish origins of the dynasties.

Fintait Mor MacNia Monarch Ireland *son of King Nia Segaman MacAmadair 86th Monarch of Ireland* – **Ireland**

Fintait Mor MacNia Monarch Ireland had one son and one daughter with MacAmadair . He died in 209. Finnat Már ("the great", later spellings Innatmar, Ionnadmhar) son of Nia Segamain, was, according to medieval Irish legend and historical tradition, a High King of Ireland. He succeeded to the throne after the death of Rudraige mac Sithrigi of plague, but after a reign of one, three or nine years he was killed by Rudraige's son.

Sabilla of Ireland *daughter of Fintait Mor MacNia Monarch Ireland* - **Meath, Leinster, Ireland**

Queen Sabilla of Ireland was born in 353 in Meath, Ireland. She married Labraidh Lorc "the Fierce" MacEnna Prince of Ireland. They had three children during their marriage. She had one brother.

Blathacht MacLabraidh King of Ireland *son of Sabilla of Ireland* - **Tara Castle, Meath, Leinster, Ancient Ireland**

Blathacht MacLabraidh King of Ireland b 340, married Magach Princess of Ireland. They had two children during their marriage. He had two brothers. He died in 280 BC

Essamain Emna Macblathachta Ireland *son of Blathacht MacLabraidh King of Ireland* - **Tara Castle, Meath, Leinster, Ancient Ireland**

Essamain Emna Macblathachta Ireland was born in 320 BC. He had one son with Magach Margaret Ireland in 300. He died in 260 BCHe had one brother.

Roignein Ruadh "The Red" MacEsamon 88th High King of Ireland *son of Essamain Emna Macblathachta Ireland* - **Tara Castle, Meath, Leinster, Ireland**

Roignein Ruadh "The Red" MacEsamon 88th High King of Ireland b 300, married Benia Ingen Criomthan Niadh Nar of Ireland. They had nine children during their marriage. He died in 240 BC Most of the country's cattle died of murrain in his time.

Fionnlogh Son Roighneim 90th High King of Ireland (187 -) *son of Roignein Ruadh "The Red" MacEsamon 88th High King of Ireland* - **Tara Castle, Meath, Leinster, Ireland**

Fionnlogh Son Roighneim 90th High King of Ireland was born in 187 to Benia Ingen Criomthan Niadh Nar of Ireland and Roignein Ruadh "The Red" MacEsamon 88th High King of Ireland. He had two sons with Benla, daughter of Creombthan of Ireland.

Fionn Macfionnloch O Henna *son of Fionnlogh Son Roighneim 90th High King of Ireland* – **Ireland**

Hill of Tara

When Fionn Macfionnloch O Henna was born in 210 his father, Fionnlogh, was 23. He married Benta Benia. They had five children during their marriage. He had four brothers.

King Eochaidh Feidhlioch *son of Fionn Macfionnloch O Henna* - **Tara Castle, Meath, Leinster,**

Ancient Castle Remains

Eochaidh Feidhlioch b 180 BC, married Clothfionn Uchtleathan. They had 13 children during their marriage. He had three brothers and one sister. He died at Tara in 130 BC

This Monarch caused the division of the Kingdom by Ugaine Mãaor into twenty-five parts, to cease; and ordered that the ancient Firvolgian division into Provinces should be resumed, viz., Two Munsters, Leinster, Conacht, and Ulster.

He also divided the government of these Provinces amongst his favourite courtiers: - Conacht he divided into three parts between Fiodhach, Eochaidh Allat, and Tinne, son of Conragh, son of Ruadhri Mãaor, No 62 on the "Line of Ir;" Ulster (Uladh) h e gave to Feargus, the son of Leighe; Leinster he gave to Ros, the son of Feargus Fairge. ; and the two Munsters he gave to Tighernach Teadhbheamach and Deagbadah.

44

After this division of the Kingdom, Eochaidh proceeded to erect a Royal Palace in Conacht; this he built on Tinne's government in a place called Druin-na-n Druagh, now Craughan (from Craughan Crodhearg, Maedhbh's mother, to whom she gave the palace), but previously, Rath Eochaidh. About the same time he bestowed his daughter the Princess Maedhbh on Tinne, whom he constituted King of Conacht; Maedhbh being hereditary Queen of that Province.

Dunguaire Castle, Hidden Gems of Connacht

After many years reign Tinne was slain by Maceacht (or Monaire) at Tara. After ten years' undivided reign, Queen Maedhbh married Oilioll Mãaor, son of Ros Ruadh, of Leinster, to whom she bore the seven Maine ; Oilioll Mãaor was at length slain by Conall Cearnach, who was soon after killed by the people of Conacht. Maedhbh was at length slain by Ferbhuidhe, the son of Conor MacNeasa (Neasa was his mother).

King Breas Nar Lotha *son of Eochaidh Feidhlioch* - **Leinster, Dublin, Ireland**

Breas Nar Lotha was born in 170 BC in Dublin, Ireland. He married Clothra Verch Eochaid. They had six children during their marriage. He had four brothers and eight sisters. He was slain at the Battle of Dram-ouach by his father.

In his time the Irish first dug graves beneath the surface to bury their dead; previously they laid the body on the surface and heaped stones over it.

Sister bears a son by her three brothers

In Irish mythology the three sons of the High King of Ireland, Eochaid Feidlech names were: Bres, Nár and Lothar. They conspired to overthrow their father. The day before meeting him in battle they were visited by their sister, Clothra, who tried in vain to dissuade them from this course of action. They were childless, so for fear that they might die without an heir, Clothra took all three of them to bed, conceiving Lugaid Riab nDerg, son of the three brothers. Lugaidh was born with (a strange thing for sure) a red circle about his neck and another about his middle. Apparently to distinguish each brother's proportion of him.

The head and face resembling Bress; the middle part between the two circles, Nar; and the downward resembling the third brother, Lothar. For which he was given the nickname of *Sriabh ndearg*, or "Red Circle" or sometimes called Lewy "of the Red Circles".

46

King Lugaidh Scriabhn Dearg of Ireland *son of Breas Nar Lotha* - **Tara Castle, Meath, Leinster,**

Lugaidh Scriabhn Dearg, 98th King of Ireland, was born in 100 BC. He married Princess Dearborguill Dervorgill Fragallsdottir and they had 14 children together. He then married Clothra verch Eochaid Feidlech of Ireland and they had 10 children together. He had five brothers.

Lughaidh Sriabh Dearg died in 0009 B.C. after having been twenty six years in the sovereignty of Ireland. It is reported he died of grief: others say he killed himself by falling upon his own sword.

Eithne ingen Lugdach Ui Itha *daughter of King Lugaidh Scriabhn Dearg of Ireland* - **Antrim,**

When Princess Eithne ingen Lugdach Uí Ítha was born in 110 her mother, Princess, was 22. She married King Mug Lama Mac Lugaid Ui Eremoin. They had six children during their marriage. She died about 150, at the age of 40.

Chapter Four

The Irish Kings of Dalriada

The earliest beginnings of the Scottish people are around the time the Romans were in Britain (55 B.C. to 409 A.D.), there were two races occupying what is today Scotland: the Picts and the Britons.

Castle Dal Riada

These Celtic peoples had successfully resisted the Roman legions, and what the Romans called Caledonia was never incorporated into the Empire. As a result, very little is known about these early inhabitants, apart from brief descriptions by Roman writers. As the Romans withdrew from Britain, these north islanders were faced with new invaders. These were the Scots from Ireland, and the Angles from Germany. It is with the Scots that we are concerned, for it is they who finally succeeded in conquering Scotland, uniting its peoples and giving them their line of kings.

49

The Scots came from a kingdom in Ireland that was known as Dalriada. This kingdom corresponded roughly with the modern County Antrim in Northern Ireland. Very little is known about the kings of Dalriada apart from their names. These are found in two medieval sources, the Book of Ballymote and the Pedigree of the Scottish Kings. It should be noted that these sources were not written contemporaneously with the events that they describe. Often, they are copies of original material which is now lost to us, and they were written centuries after the fact.

The Dalriada crossed the North Channel from Ireland to Kintyre in Scotland, eventually establishing a kingdom around Argyll. The first record of this migration is in 258 A.D., when the Romans noted that Scots from the north attacked south as far as London. In time, the Dalriadan kingdom in Scotland overshadowed that in Ireland, and the kings made their home in Argyll, in its ancient capital of Dunadd. Around the year 500 A.D., the two sons of Erc, Fergus and Loarn, were kings of Dalriada in Scotland.

Fiachra Cathmail MacEochaid Irish Dalriada *son of Eithne ingen Lugdach Ui Itha -* **Antrim,**

When Fiachra Cathmail MacEochaid Irish Dalriada was born in 120 in Antrim, Antrim, Northern Ireland, his father, King Mug Lama Mac Lugaid Ui Eremoin, was 33 and his mother, Princess, Eithne ingen Lugdach Uí Ítha was 20.
He had two sons with Sarad Ingen Conn
He died in 165 in Antrim, at 93.

Eochaid Antoit MacFIACHRACH King of Irish Dalriada *son of Fiachra Cathmail MacEochaid Irish Dalriada -* **Dalriada, Northeastern Ireland**

When Eochaid Antoit MacFIACHRACH King of Irish Dalriada was born in 144 his father, Fiachra, was 24 and his mother, Sarad, was 24. He had three sons with Mongain Finn NicFideach Ohailill between 120 and 168. He died in 186 in Somme, Picardie, France, at the age of 42.

King Achir Cirre MacEchach *son of Eochaid Antoit MacFIACHRACH King of Irish Dalriada -* **Dalriada, Northeastern Ireland**

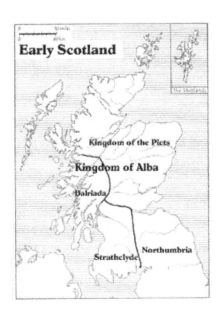

When King Achir Cirre MacEchach was born in 168 his father, Eochaid, was 24. He had one son. He died in 275 in Somme, Picardie, France, at the age of 107.

His son King Finn Fiacc O Conaire was born in 192 in Antrim, Northern Ireland.

Coat of Arms, Ireland, Irish Celtic

Celtic knots are perhaps the most notorious and recognizable

artwork in Celtic history. They started appearing in history after about 450 AD; the Celtic knots meaning is sketchy at best, because there is little written history documenting their purpose. Repetition of their appearance through history in conjunction with other various human interpretations give us insight, and allow us to infer some basic information relating to the Celtic knots meaning. The Celtic knot symbol, is also referred to as the mystic knot, or the endless knot

---

King Finn Fiacc O Conaire MacAchir of Irish DalRiata *son of*

King Achir Cirre MacEchach -
Dalriada, Ireland

King Finn Fiacc O Conaire MacAchir of Irish DalRiata was born in 192 in Antrim, Antrim, Northern Ireland, the child of King Achir Cirre. He had two sons. He died in Antrim, Antrim, Northern Ireland. He fought in battle against Dadera, the Druid; Neimhidh, son of Sroibhcinn whom he killed in revenge for his father; and the south of Ireland in 186 at the Battle of Ceannfeabhrat

Cruithluithe MacFinn King of Dal Riata Ireland *son of King Finn Fiacc O Conaire MacAchir of Irish DalRiata* - **Dalriada, Antrim, Ulster, Northeastern Ireland**

When Cruithluithe MacFinn King of Dal Riata Ireland was born in 216 his father, was 24. He had two sons and one daughter with his Wife. He died in Somme, Picardie, France.

Wife of Senchormac MacCruithluithe King of Irish Dal Riata *daughter of Cruithluithe MacFinn King of Dal Riata Ireland* - **Dalriada, Antrim, Ulster, Northeastern Ireland**

When Senchormac MacCruithluithe King of Irish Dal Riata's wife was born in 240 her father, Cruithluithe, was 24 and her mother, was 23. She had two sons and one daughter between 234 and 272. She died in Somme, Picardie, France.

Wife of Felim Romaich King Of Dal Riata daughter *of Wife of Senchormac MacCruithluithe King of Irish Dal Riata* - **Dalriada, Antrim, Northeastern Ireland**

When Felim Romaich King Of Dal Riata's wife was born in 272 in Antrim, Northern Ireland, her mother was 32. She had five sons with Felim Romaich Ruamnach MacSENCHORMAC King of Dal Riata. She had two brothers.

Áengus Buiding Mac Feideilmid King of Irish Dal Riata son *of Wife of Felim Romaich King Of Dal Riata -* **Dalriada, Antrim, Ulster,**

When Áengus Buiding Mac Feideilmid King of Irish Dal Riata was born in 280 in Ringkobing, Denmark, his father, Felim, was 26 and his mother, was 18. He had one son with Aengus Buiding (Buaidnech) MacFEIDEILMID MacFEIDEILMID . He then married Fincormach Picts and they had four children together. He had four brothers.

Fedelmid Aislingich the Aisling MacAengusa, King Of Irish Dalriada *son of Áengus Buiding Mac Feideilmid King of Irish Dal Riata* - **Dalriada**

Feargusa Castle

Fedelmid Aislingich the Aisling MacAengusa, King of Irish Dalriada was born in 312 in Ringkobing, Denmark, the child of Áengus Buiding Mac Feideilmid and Aengus Buiding (Buaidnech) MacFEIDEILMID . He had three sons. He died in 405 in Argyll, at the age of 93.

Aongus Fertas the Foutunat MacFedelmid King Dal Riata son *of Fedelmid Aislingich the Aisling MacAengusa, King Of Irish Dalriada* - **Dalriada, Antrim, Ulster, Northeastern Ireland**

Ulster Flag

When Aongus Fertas the Foutunat MacFedelmid King Dal Riata was born in 350 his father, Fedelmid, was 38. He had three sons and two daughters with Fogan Owen between 370 and 380. He died in 439 having lived 89 years.

Eochaidh Muinreamhar MacAongus, King of Dalriada *son of Aongus Fertas the Foutunat MacFedelmid King Dal Riata* - **Dalriada, Antrim, Ulster, Ireland**

When Eochaidh Muinreamhar MacAongus, King of Dalriada was born in 370 in Antrim, Antrim, Northern Ireland, his father, Aongus, was 20 and his mother, Fogan, was 39. He married Loarn Erca in 423. They had two children during their marriage. He died in 445 having lived 75 years.

Ercc - Earc MacEochaid King of Irish Dal Riata *son of Eochaidh Muinreamhar MacAongus, King of Dalriada* -

Dalriada, Antrim, Ulster, Ireland

When Ercc - Earc MacEochaid King of Irish Dal Riata was born in 400 his father, Eochaidh, was 30 and his mother, Loarn, was 30. He was married three times and had 14 sons. He died in 474 at the age of 74.

Erc is significant as he has been traditionally regarded as the ancestor, through his son Fergus Mor, of the kings of Dalriada, and **through them the Kings of Scotland,**

Chapter Five

From Ireland into Scotland

The Scots were originally the Irish of Ulster, some of whom moved to Argyll. The *Scoti* of Scotland came from Ireland. "Scotus" was the Latin word for Irishman—or at least the tribes in and near the northern part of county Antrim, and probably all of northeastern Ulster. The tribes of Ireland in Ulster, especially the Dal Riada, gave Scotland its name:

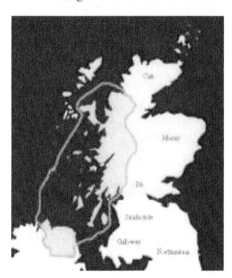

"It has been stated that the kingship of Dal Riata was moved to Scotland with Fergus mac Earca and his descendants, and that later in the 6th century the lords of the Dal Riata in Ireland were also allied with their southern neighbors, the Dal Fiatach." Ancient Uladh— Kingdom of Ulster—Uladh, from Ireland's History in Maps.

Confirmation that the Irish of Dalriada were the Scoti who settled in Scotland as early as the fourth century, and eventually gave Scotland its name, is found in Settlement on the Western Seaboard c. AD300-800: Dalriada and North Uist by Ewan J. Innes 1993:

"The Scots of Dalriada were originally from Ireland, from an

57

*area along the Antrim coast and part of the province of Ulster
(now counties Antrim and Down). The originator of the political
territory of the Dál Riata in Scotland was Fergus Mór mac Eirc
who arrived in Kintyre c. 500.*

*"When Fergus Mór removed from Ireland to Scotland, there was
no sundering of ties or relinquishing of authority between the two
sections; and this continued to be the case under Fergus Mór's
successors. Evidence for the continued rule of Dál Riata in
Ireland by the Scottish branch is found at the Convention of
Druim Cett. This was convened c. 575 to discuss the future
relations and status of the Irish Dál Riata between Aed, son of
Ainmire (d. 598) the leader of the Northern Uí Néill—the most
powerful people in the north of Ireland at the time—and Aedán
mac Gabráin king of Dál Riata in Scotland (d. c. 608)."*

*"Many authors testify that Scota was the name of Ireland, and
that it was the Irish who were called the Scotic race. Thus does
Jonas the abbot, in the second chapter, treating of Columcille,
speak: 'Colman,' he says, who is called Colum, was born in
Hibernia, which is inhabited by the Scotic race.' Beda also in the
first chapter of the first book of the History of Sacsa, says that
Ireland was the native land of the Scots. He speaks thus:
'Hibernia is the true fatherland of the Scots.'*

*The same author, writing about the saints, makes a remark which
agrees with this: 'It was from Hibernia, the island of the Scots,
that St. Kilian and his two companions came.' From this it is to be
inferred that the Irish were called the Scotic race in the time of
Beda, who lived 700 years after Christ. ... The truth of this matter
will be seen from the words of Capgrave, writing of St. Colum; he
speaks thus: 'Scotia was an ancient name of Ireland, whence came
the Scotic race, who inhabit that part of Alba which lies nearest to
greater Britain; and that Alba is now for this reason, called
Scotia from Ireland, from which they derive their origin, and
whence they immediately came.'"*

Keating cites many other early writings demonstrating that Ireland
was regularly referred to as Scotia in the first millennium. For
example, from the Serarius of St. Boniface: "There are, however,
two Scotias: one of them, the elder and proper Scotia, is Ireland,
and the other in northern Britain."

Fergus Mór, the Great MacEarca 1st King of Scottish Dal Riata
son of Ercc - Earc MacEochaid King of Irish Dal Riata -

Dalriada, Scotia now Argyll, Scotland

When Fergus Mór, the Great MacEarca 1st King of Scottish Dal Riata was born on June 29, 0430, in Argyll, his father, Ercc, was 30 and his mother, Misi, was 18. He had one son and one daughter with Feldelm Foltchain - Fedelmia Queen of DALRIADA. He then married Wrold Av Pictland and they had four children together. He died on October 12, 0501, in Iona, Argyll, at the age of 71.

Fergus brought *Jacob's Pillar a/k/a The Stone of Destiny* with him from Ireland when he established Scotland. This is the celebrated Stone of Scone now in the Coronation Chair in Westminster Abbey.

Some believe Fergus can claim lineage to **King Arthur**. The succession of early Scottish kings is complicated by the custom of passing the crown between different branches of the dynasty in succeding generations. In an age when kings frequently died by violence comparatively young this custom ensured that the crown was likely to be inherited by a mature man rather than a child.

Rulers of Scotland from Cináed mac Ailpín until the present time claim descent from Fergus Mór.

Domangart I Dungardus, Treacherous King of Dalraida MacFergus *son of Fergus Mór, the Great MacEarca 1st King of Scottish Dal Riata* - **Dunolly Castle, Dunadd, Dalriada, Argyllshire, Scotland**

Dunolly Castle

When Domangart I Dungardus, Treacherous King of Dalraida MacFergus was born in 465 in Argyll, his father, Fergus, was 35 and his mother, Wrold, was 5.

He married Fedlim The Fair of Ireland Queen of Dalraida Connaught in 489. He then married Domangart Feldelm Foltchain, daughter of Brion son of Eochaid Mugmedon, a half-brother to the High King of Ireland Niall of the Nine Hostages. He has at two sons: Comgall and Gabhran, who became kings in succession.

The Tripartite Life of St. Patrick states that he was present at the death of the saint, circa 493. Domangart died around 507 and was succeeded by Comgall. He died in 534 in Argyll, at the age of 69.

Dunollie Castle is a small ruin located on a hill north of the town of Oban, on the west coast Scotland. It commands a view of the town, harbour and, outlying isles. The ruin is accessible by a short, steep path. There has been a fortification on this high promontory since the days of the kingdom of Dál Riata.

Gabran Gabhran Argyll Treacherous 4th King of Dalriada MacDomangart *son of Domangart I Dungardus, Treacherous King of Dalraida MacFergus* - **Dunolly Castle, Dunadd, Dalriada, Argyllshire, Scotland**

When Gabran Gabhran Argyll Treacherous 4th King ofDalriada MacDomangart was born in 490 in Argyll, his father, Domangart, was 25 and his mother, Feldelm, was 15. He married Lleian Ingenach verch Brychan of Queen of Dalriada and Scotland. They had nine children during their marriage. He died in 560 at the age of 70.

Aedan macGabhran Argyil King of Dalraida and Scotland *son of Gabran Gabhran Argyll Treacherous 4th King ofDalriada MacDomangart* - **Dunolly Castle, Dunadd, Dalriada, Argyllshire, Scotland**

When Aedan macGabhran Argyil King of Dalraida and Scotland was born in 532 in Argyll, his father, Gabran, was 42 and his mother, Lleian, was 32. He had 19 sons and one daughter.

In 575, Aedan attended the Convention of Druim Cet in Ireland, which apparently convened to decide the political relationship between Dalriada and the kings of northern Ui Neill in Ireland, whose power was growing. In 581, he led an expedition to the Orkney Isles, and he won a victory at the Isle of Man in the following year.

In 590, he won a battle against the Maetae, his British neighbors, but lost two of his sons (Eochaid Find and Artur) in the battle. In 596, in the first battle between the Scots and English, two more of his sons (Bran and Domangart) were slain. In 600, he led an army against the English of Northumbria, but was decisively defeated at Degsatan. He was victorious in a battle against the Picts sometime between 596 and 606

The Irish annals record Áedán's campaigns against his neighbors, in Ireland, and in northern Britain, including the east coast of Scotland. As recorded by Bede, Áedán was decisively defeated by Æthelfrith of Bernicia at the Battle of Degsastan.

Æthelfrith had won many victories against the Britons and was expanding his power and territory, and this concerned Áedán, who led "an immense and mighty army" against Æthelfrith. Although Æthelfrith had the smaller army, almost all of Áedán's army was slain, and Áedán himself fled. After this defeat the Irish kings in Britain would not make war against the English again. Áedán may have been deposed, or have abdicated, following this defeat. His date of death is recorded as 17 April 609.

Eochaidh I Buidhe MacAedan "The Yellow Haired" "The Red" King of Dalraida and Scotland *son of Aedan macGabhran Argyil King of Dalraida and Scotland -* **Dunolly Castle, Dunadd, Dalriada, Argyllshire, Scotl**

Dunolly Castle

When Eochaidh I Buidhe MacAedan "The Yellow Haired" "The Red" King of Dalraida and Scotland was born in 570 in Argyll, his father, Aedan, was 38 and his mother was 37.

He married Thurida, Princess of Mumhan and they had 12 children together. He also married Fergusa of Delradia Princess Royal of Picts Queen of Scotland Urgusia in Argyll. He died in 630 in Argyll, at the age of 60.

He is often referred to as King of the Picts or King of the Scots.

Domnall Breac 'The Speckled' MacEochaid King of Dalraida and Scotland *son of Eochaidh I Buidhe MacAedan "The Yellow Haired" "The Red" King of Dalraida and Scotland* - **Dalrida, Argyll, Argyllshire, Scotland**

When Domnall Breac 'The Speckled' MacEochaid King of Dalraida and Scotland was born in 600 in Argyll, his father, Eochaidh, was 30 and his mother, Thurida,, Princess was 21. He had 12 sons. He died in Strathcarron, Ross-shire, at the age of 43.

He was king of Dál Riata, from about 629 until 642. He at the 622 battle of Cend Delgthen (probably in the east midlands of Ireland) as an ally of Conall Guthbinn of Clann Cholmáin. This is the only battle known where Domnall Brecc fought on the winning side.

Domnall suffered four defeats after he broke Dál Riata's alliance with the Cenél Conaill clan of the Uí Néill. In Ireland, Domnall and his ally Congal Cáech of the Dál nAraidi were defeated by Domnall mac Áedo of the Cenél Conaill, the High King of Ireland, at the Battle of Mag Rath (Moira, County Down) in 637. He also lost to the Picts in 635 and 638 and lastly to Eugein I of Alt Clut at Strathcarron in 642, where he was killed.

Domangart mac Domnaill II King of Scotland *son of Domnall Breac 'The Speckled' MacEochaid King of Dalraida and Scotland* - **Dunolly Castle, Dunadd, Dalriada, Argyllshire, Scotland**

When Domangart mac Domnaill King of Scotland was born in 630 in Argyll, his father, Domnall, was 30. He had one son with More Mumhan Scotland. He then married Inconnu, Princess of the Picts, De Picts Leainftech and they had four children together. He died in 673 in Argyll, at the age of 43.

Findon (Eochaid) II "Crook-Nose" MacDongart King of Scotland *son of Domangart mac Domnaill II King of Scotland* **Dunolly Castle, Dunadd, Dalriada, Argyllshire, Scotland**

When Eochaid II Crooked nose Mac Domangart King of Dal Riada was born in 658 in Argyll, his father, Domangart, was 28 and his mother, Inconnu, was 18. He married Spondana of Picts and they had 18 children together. He also married Macechdach Lochaber Dalriada. He died in 698 at the age of 40.

Eochaid Angbaid MacEchach Argyll Dalriada *son of Findon (Eochaid) II "Crook-Nose" MacDongart King of Scotland -*

Dunolly Castle, Dunadd, Dalriada, Argyllshire, Scotland

When Eochaid Angbaid MacEchach Argyll Dalriada was born in 690 in Argyll, his father, Findon, was 32 and his mother, Spondana, was 23. He married Macechdach Lochaber Dalriada and they had nine children together. He then had two sons with WROLD Verch Fereduc of the Picts Dalaoda . He died in 733 in Argyll, at the age of 43.

Fergus II Wrguist Urgust Ungust MacEchach na Oriel King of

Dalriada *son of Eochaid Angbaid MacEchach Argyll Dalriada* – **Dunolly Castle, Scotland**

When Fergus II Wrguist Urgust Ungust MacEchach na Oriel King of Dalriada was born in 727, his father, Eochaid, was 37. He married Feredach Wrold and they had four children together. He also married Wrold Av Pictland. He died in 781 at 54 years.

Fergusa Urgusia Royal Picts of Scotland *daughter of Fergus II Wrguist Urgust Ungust MacEchach na Oriel King of Dalriada -* **Dunolly Castle, Dunadd, Dalriada, Argyllshire, Scotland**

When Fergusa Urgusia Royal Picts of Scotland was born in 755 in Argyll, her father, Fergus, was 28 and her mother, Feredach, was 35. She had 22 sons. She died in 803 in Argyll, at the age of 48.

Alpin Kintyre Scotland MacEochaid *son of Fergusa Urgusia Royal Picts of Scotland -* **Dunolly Castle, Dunadd, Dalriada**

When Alpin Kintyre Scotland MacEochaid was born in 778 in Fordoun, Kincardineshire, his father, Argyll, was 31 and his mother, Fergusa, was 23. He had six sons and seven daughters. He died on July 20, 0836, at the age of 59.

The Ruins of Galloway Castle

Alpin is said to have caused complete destruction of Galloway before being killed there in 836. His actions led to the merger of the Kingdom of the Scots with the Kingdom of the Picts, with the Picts victorious.

Kenneth I (Cinaed) MacAlpine Picts Scotland *son of Alpin Kintyre Scotland MacEochaid* - **Iona, Argyllshire, Scotland**

When Kenneth I (Cinaed) MacAlpine Picts Scotland was born in 810 in Iona, Argyll, his father, Alpin, was 32 and his mother, Unuisticc, was 28. He married Nicdonhnull the Isles in 830 in Iona, Argyll. They had 31 children during their marriage. He died on February 13, 0859, in Perth, Perthshire, at the age of 49.

Kenneth King of the Picts

Kenneth's rise can be placed in the context of the recent end of the previous dynasty, which had dominated Fortriu for two or four generations.

This followed the death of king Uen son of Óengus of Fortriu, his brother Bran, Áed mac Boanta "and others almost innumerable" in battle against the Vikings in 839. The resulting succession crisis seems, to have resulted in at least four would-be kings warring for supreme power.

It is reported that Kenneth held a banquet at Scone after his succession and murdered seven earls of Dalriada and others who might have disputed his succession.

Kenneth's reign is dated from 843, during which he was involved in innumerable battles against the Vikings. It was not until 848 that he defeated the last of his rivals for power. The Pictish Chronicle claims that he was king in Dál Riata for two years before becoming Pictish king in 843.

In 849, Kenneth had many sacred items of Columba, which may have included the Monymusk Reliquary, transferred from Iona to Dunkeld. Other than these bare facts, the Chronicle of the Kings of Alba reports that he invaded *Saxonia* six times, captured Melrose and burnt Dunbar, and also that Vikings laid waste to Pictland, reaching far into the interior.

On his death in 858 in Forteviot, Kenneth was buried on Iona. Kenneth's brother became King Donald I. Described at the time as "the wanton son of the foreign woman" Donald extended Dalriadic law into Pictland and died of natural causes near Scone, Perthshire in 862.

Of Kenneth's five children, two later became kings - Constantine I who took over on the death of King Donald I, ruled from 862 to 878 and was killed in a battle fighting the Danes. Another son, Aedh (who

Dunnottar Castle

reigned from 878 to 879) was killed by his cousin Giric, a son of Donald I. Kenneth's three daughters married well - to the King Run of Strathclyde (laying the foundation of a further extension of Alba), the Norwegian King of Dublin and the High King of Ireland, Aedh Finnlaith.

Constantine I of Alba King of Scotland *son of Kenneth I (Cinaed) MacAlpine Picts Scotland* - **Forteviot, Perthshire, , Scotland**

When Constantine I of Alba King of Scotland was born in 836 in Forteviot, Perthshire, his father, Kenneth, was 26 and his mother, Nicdonhnull, was 22. He married Princess Sabhdh of Alba and they had four children together.

He then had one son with Thurid Eyvindsdatter. He also married Queen Constantine of Scotland in Fife. Constantine died in 877 at the age of 41.

He succeeded his uncle Donald I mac Ailpín as Pictish king following the latter's death on 13 April 862. Constantine I's reign witnessed increased activity by Vikings, based in Ireland, Northumbria and northern Britain as he died fighting one such invasion. Viking activity in northern Britain appears to have reached a peak during his reign. Viking armies were led by a small group of men who may have been his kinsmen.

In 875 a Viking army invades and a battle is fought near Dollar. It was a heavy defeat for the Picts; the *Annals of Ulster* say that "a great slaughter of the Picts resulted". In 877, shortly after building a new church at St Andrews, He was captured and executed by Viking raiders. Although there is agreement on the time and general manner of his death, it is generally believed he was beheaded on a beach at Fife.

Donald II Dasachtach Scotland *son of Constantine I of Alba King of Scotland* - **Forres, Moray, Fordoun, Kincardineshire, Scotland**

When Donald II Dasachtach Scotland was born about 862, in Fordoun, Kincardineshire, his father, Constantine, was 26 and his mother, Princess, was 32. He was married three times and had six sons and three daughters. He died in 900 at the age of 38.

Donald became king on the death or deposition of King Giric mac Dúngail in about 889. Donald's death is dated to 900 by the Annals of Ulster and the Chronicon Scotorum, where he is called *king of Alba*, rather than *king of the Picts*.

The Chronicle of the Kings of Alba reports:
Doniualdus son of Constantini held the kingdom for 11 years [889–900]. The Northmen wasted Pictland at this time. In his reign a battle occurred between Danes and Scots at Innisibsolian where the Scots had victory. He was killed at Opidum Fother [modern Dunnottar] by the Gentiles.

He was buried on the Isle of Iona. The change from *king of the Picts* to *king of Alba* is seen as indicating a step towards the kingdom of the Scots The "Chronicle of the Kings of Alba" has Donald succeeded by his cousin Constantine II. Donald's son Malcolm (Máel Coluim mac Domnall) was later king as Malcolm I.

Malcolm I King Of Scotland *son of Donald II Dasachtach Scotland* - **Fordoun, Kincardineshire, Grampian, Scotland**

When Malcolm I King Of Scotland was born in 895 in Fordoun, Kincardineshire, his father, Donald, was 33 and his mother, Sigurd, was 29. He had 19 sons and 16 daughters. He died in 995 in Fordoun, Kincardineshire, at the age of 100.

He became king when his cousin King Constantine II abdicated to become a monk. In 945, King Edmund I of England, having expelled King Olaf Sihtricsson from Northumbria, devastated the lands of Cumbria and blinded the two sons of Domnall mac Eógain, king of Strathclyde. It is said that he then ceded Strathclyde to King Malcolm in return for an alliance.

King Malcolm appears to have kept his agreement with the now late King Edmund I. This agreement apparently was renewed with the new English king, King Edred, his brother Edmund having been murdered.

In 949–950, king Malcolm I raided Northumbria as far south as the Tees taking "a multitude of people and many herds of cattle" according to the Chronicle. The Annals of Ulster for the year 952 report a battle between "the men of Alba and the Britons [of Strathclyde] and the English" against the foreigners, i.e. the Northmen or the Norse-Gaels. King Malcolm was killed in 954 probably at the battle for Mearns. He was buried on Iona. His sons Dub and Cináed were later kings.

Kenneth II Kings of Scots- House of Alpin MacMalcolm King of Scotland, King of Alba, King of Lothain son *of Malcolm I King Of Scotland* - **Iona, Argyllshire, Scotland**

When Kenneth II, Kings of Scots-House of Alpin MacMalcolm was born on June 4, 0932, in Iona, Argyll, his father, Malcolm, was 37. He married Lady Aelgigu Edith, Queen of Scotland, Princess of Leinster O Muiredaig about 949, in Kincardineshire. They had 13 children during their marriage. He died on March 25, 995, in Fettercairn, Kincardineshire, at the age of 62. Kenneth II of Scotland (reigned 971-995) attempted to change the succession rules, allowing "*the nearest survivor in blood to the deceased king to succeed*", thus securing the throne for his own descendants. He reportedly did so to specifically exclude Constantine (III) and Kenneth (III). Learning of this Constantine and Kenneth then jointly conspired against him, convincing Finnguala, daughter of Cuncar, Mormaer of Angus, to kill the king. She reportedly did so to achieve personal revenge, as Kenneth II had killed her own son.

The Plotting and Revenge Killing of a King
In the account of John of Fordun, Constantine the Bald, son of King Cullen and Gryme were "plotting unceasingly the death of the king and his son".
The story. . .
One day, Kenneth II and his companions went hunting into the woods, "at no great distance from his own abode". The hunt took him to Fettercairn, a small village in Aberdeenshire, where Lady Finella resided.

She approached him to proclaim her loyalty and invited him to visit her residence, whispering into his ear that she had information about a conspiracy plot. She managed to lure him to "an out-of-the-way little cottage", where a booby trap was hidden. Inside the cottage was a statue, connected by strings to a number of crossbows.

Fettercairn, where King Kenneth II was assassinated

If anyone touched or moved the statue, he would trigger the crossbows and fall victim to their arrows. Kenneth II gently touched the statue and "was shot though by arrows sped from all sides, and fell without uttering another word." Lady Finella escaped through the woods and managed to join her co-conspirators, Constantine III and Gryme.

The hunting companions soon discovered the bloody king. They first searched for Finalla and, unable to locate her, proceeded to burn the village of Fettercairn to the ground.

King of Scotland Malcolm II *son of Kenneth II, Kings of Scots-House of Alpin MacMalcolm King of Scotland, King of Alba, King of Lothain -* **Athol, Perth, Perthshire, Scotland**

When King of Scotland Malcolm II was born in 958 in Perth, Perthshire, his father, Kenneth, was 26 and his mother, Lady, was 26. He married Edith Aefgifu Aelgifu, Sigundsodottir Queen of Scotland Ossary DeOssory and they had 26 children together. He then married Hvarflad, Queen of Scotland Hlodversdatter Queen of Scotland and they had two children together. He died on November 25, 1034, having lived 76 years.

It is reported that Malcolm defeated a Norwegian army "in almost the first days after his coronation". The Dioceses of Mortlach (later moved to Aberdeen) was founded in thanks for this victory over the Norwegians. In 1005 at the battle of Monzievaird in Strathearn he killed King Constantine's successor Kenneth III.

Malcolm died 25 November 1034 at Glamis, a small village in Angus, Scotland. Many described him as a "most glorious" or "most victorious" king of Scotland.

Perhaps the most notable feature of Malcolm's death is the account of Marianus, matched by the silence of the Irish annals, which tells us that Duncan I became king and ruled for five years and nine months. Given that his death in 1040 is described as being "at an immature age" in the Annals of Tigernach, he must have been a young man in 1034. The absence of any opposition suggests that Malcolm had dealt thoroughly with any likely opposition in his own lifetime.

Tradition knew the Pictish stone now called "Glamis 2" as "King Malcolm's grave stone". The stone was apparently formed by re-using a Bronze Age standing stone dating from the 8th century. He is not buried here but rather at Iona. It is believed that the stone marks the spot where he fell in battle.

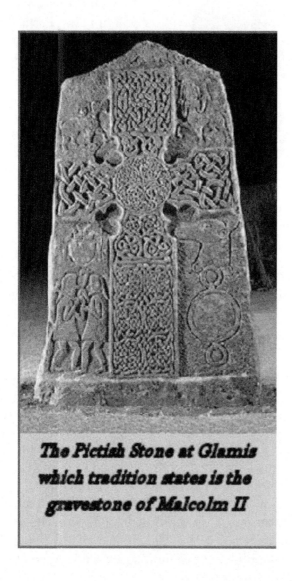

The Pictish Stone at Glamis which tradition states is the gravestone of Malcolm II

Chapter Six

On to France – Norman Knights

On to France where we mixed with the Normans - descendants of those Vikings, or Norsemen, who settled in northern France (or the Frankish kingdom). The Normans founded the duchy of

Normandy and sent out expeditions of conquest and colonization to southern Italy and Sicily and to England, Wales, Scotland, and Ireland.

The Normans were originally pagan barbarian pirates from Denmark, Norway, and Iceland who began to make destructive plundering raids on European coastal settlements in the 8th century. During the later 9th century their raids on the northern and western coastlands of France grew in scale and frequency, and the Vikings had secured a permanent foothold on Frankish soil in the valley of the lower Seine River by about 900. A Viking named Rollo, who had already won a reputation as a great leader of Viking raiders in Scotland and Ireland, soon emerged as the outstanding personality among the new settlers.

In 911 the Frankish king Charles III the Simple made the Treaty of St. Clair-sur-Epte with Rollo, ceding him the land around the mouth of the Seine and what is now the city of Rouen. Within a generation the Vikings, or Normans, as they came to be known, had extended their rule westward to the districts of Lower Normandy. From then on until the mid-11th century, the history of the Normans in Normandy was marked by a line of ruthless and forceful rulers calling themselves counts, or dukes, of Normandy and struggling to establish political hegemony over the indigenous Frankish population of the region.

Despite their eventual conversion to Christianity, their adoption of the French language, and their abandonment of sea roving for

Frankish cavalry warfare in the decades following their settlement in Normandy, the Normans retained many of the traits of their piratical Viking ancestors.

They displayed an extreme restlessness and recklessness, a love of fighting accompanied by almost foolhardy courage, and a craftiness and cunning that went hand in hand with outrageous treachery. In their expansion into other parts of Europe, the Normans compiled a record of astonishingly daring exploits in which often a mere handful of men would vanquish an enemy many times as numerous.

An unequaled capacity for rapid movement across land and sea, the use of brutal violence, a precocious sense of the use and value of money—these are among the traits traditionally assigned to the Normans.

From their settlements in Normandy the adventurous Normans embarked on several major expansionary campaigns in Europe. The most important of these was the invasion of England in 1066 by William, duke of Normandy (Cousin Willim the Conqueror), who became king of England upon the success of what is now known as the Norman Conquest.

William the Conqueror Battle of Hastings

Early in the 11th century Norman adventurers also began a somewhat more prolonged and haphazard migration to southern Italy and Sicily, where they served the local nobility as mercenaries fighting the Arabs and the Byzantines. As more Normans arrived, they carved out small principalities for themselves from their former employers.

Among the most remarkable of these Norman adventurers were the sons of Tancred de Hauteville, who established their rule over the southern Italian regions of Calabria and Puglia (Apulia) in the 1050s and over Sicily in the following decades.

Roger II, a grandson of Tancred, amalgamated their possessions in the early 12th century as the kingdom of Sicily, whose rulers retained a basically Norman character until the last decades of that century.

The art of building castles was not a Norman invention, but the Normans became masters in the use of the simple yet enormously effective motte-and-bailey castle—a mound (motte) topped by a timber palisade and tower, surrounded by a ditched and palisaded enclosure (bailey). These little fortifications, which were complementary to the warfare conducted in open country by small units of cavalry, became the hallmark of Norman penetration and conquest.

Again, although the Normans were at first novices and imitators in the practice of fighting on horseback, they soon became masters of cavalry warfare as it was then practiced in continental Europe.

Norman Knights riding in close order

Mounted on much the same breed of war horse as his Frankish, Angevin, or Breton opponent, wearing the heavy mail hauberk that was standard among the warriors of northwestern Europe, protected by a conical helmet and a kite-shaped shield, and armed with a long, broad-bladed sword and a slender lance, the Norman cavalryman proved on countless occasions that he could outfight and overwhelm the most powerful forces brought against him.

Among the Norman traits regarded by their contemporaries as especially characteristic were their utterly unbridled character and their capacity for quick and fruitful imitation and adaptation. The former characteristic contributed to the production, by a process akin to natural selection, of lines of outstandingly able and ruthless rulers wherever a Norman state came into being. Many of the early Norman rulers of Normandy, England, and Sicily were among the most powerful and successful secular potentates of their age in Western Europe in their ability to create political institutions that were both stable and enduring.

The Normans' capacity for imitation and adaptation was even more significant for the history of Europe. The Normans began as pagan destroyers bent upon plundering and slaughter.

Forced to come to terms with the Carolingian and Capetian dynasties and to adopt French as their language and Christianity as their religion, they quickly became missionaries and proselytizers of the civilization that they had attacked and that had ultimately absorbed them. They quickly grasped the principles of Carolingian feudalism and Normandy became a highly feudalized state.

Just as the Normans became the typical exponents of Carolingian feudalism and of cavalry and castle warfare, so they also became in part the exponents and champions of religious orthodoxy. Under the patronage of the ducal house of Normandy, religious life in the province flourished, and a number of Norman monasteries became renowned centers of Benedictine life and learning. This was chiefly due to the encouragement given to non-Norman scholars and reformers to make their home in Normandy.

The great religious and ecclesiastical revival that marks 11th-

Norman Monastery

century Normandy found another expression in the popularity among the Normans of pilgrimages to Rome and to the Holy Land. This yearning for pilgrimages was one of the factors responsible for the Norman conquest of southern Italy. Many Norman nobles journeyed to the Mediterranean inspired by a naive mixture of religious devotion, a love of adventure, and a desire for fresh conquests. Surprisingly, though, the part played by the Normans in the early Crusades was relatively slight, consisting chiefly of the erection of the short-lived principality of Antioch by Norman nobles in the 12th century.

The Normans were quick to imitate whatever they saw, and this faculty of imitation is evident in all the different countries where the Normans settled. But Norman imitation was never slavish, and is certainly not the whole story of Norman achievement.

A truer explanation of Norman success would be that they combined a boundless self-confidence with a marked capacity for adapting to their own purposes the institutions they found in newly won territories. Thus, in Puglia and Sicily their control was based on faith in their own military superiority, their strategic use of castles and harbors, and their importation of feudalism to govern the relations of the count or king with his more important subjects. In government, however, they adopted the highly advanced and largely literate techniques already developed by the Byzantine Greeks and the Muslims.

Norman Knight

In England the Normans similarly brought their own brand of feudalism and their own ideas of strong personal government and fiscal institutions. But there too they adopted many of the existing institutions and customs.

Even at the end of Henry I's reign (1135) in England the whole structure of royal government remained fundamentally Anglo-Saxon— monarchy, king's council, royal seal and writing office, the shire system and the sheriffs, the twofold revenue system consisting of the produce of royal estates compounded into annual cash payments and a direct tax levied on the landowning class, all originated before the Norman Conquest.

But under Norman direction, and with a number of Norman innovations such as the exchequer, the itinerant justices, and the sworn inquest, this system worked much more efficiently after 1066 than before, and, a fact of equal importance, England was made safe from foreign invasion.

Doda 'Duxia', Princess-Scotland De Scotland *daughter of King of Scotland Malcolm II* - **Falaise, Calvados, Basse-Normandie, France**

Doda 'Duxia', Princess-Scotland De Scotland was born in 973 Glamis Castle in Angus, Forfarshire, Scotland the child of King of Scotland and Queen Edith Aelgifu. She married Fulbert DeFalaise in 1000. They had 28 children during their marriage. She died at Falaise, Basse-Normandie, France.

Grandmother of William the Conqueror

She and her husband, Fulbert of Falaise, were the parents of Herleva, mother of the illegitimate William the Conqueror, the 11th-century Duke of Normandy and King of England.[1]

Reynald Lord Of Croy de Grai *son of Doda 'Duxia', Princess-Scotland De Scotland* - **Falaise, Calvados, Basse-Normandie, France**

When Reynald Lord Of Croy de Grai was born in 1008 in Falaise, Basse-Normandie, France, his father, Fulbert, was 35. He married Mrs-Reynald de Falaise and they had five children together. He then had one son from another relationship. He then married Herleva Arlete Arlotta Herleve DeFalaise in 1032 in Croix, Nord-Pas-de-Calais, France. Reynald died in 1058 in Croix, Nord-Pas-de-Calais, France, at the age of 50. **Related to President George Washington**

John I De Grai (Grey), Count of Croix (Croy), Norman Knight
son of Reynald Lord Of Croy de Grai - **Croy, Piccardy,
Normandy, France**

When John I De Grai (Grey), Count of Croix (Croy), Norman
Knight was born about 1033, in France, his father, Reynald, was
25 and his mother, Mrs-Reynald, was 23.

He married Adeliza FitzOsbern, Countess of Croy in 1056 in
France. They had five children during their marriage. He died in
1080 in France, at the age of 47.

John De Crai's Tomb

Cousin William the Conqueror's Great Adventure

William was of Viking origin. Though he spoke a dialect of French and grew up in Normandy, a fiefdom loyal to the French kingdom, he and other Normans descended from Scandinavian invaders. One of William's relatives, Rollo, pillaged northern France with fellow Viking raiders in the late ninth and early 10th centuries, eventually accepting his own territory (Normandy, named for the Norsemen who controlled it) in exchange for peace.

Norman Knights

William the Conqueror was the Duke of Normandy, and already recognized as the greatest warrior of his age when he landed a fleet at Hastings, and conquered the Saxon kingdom of England. In defeating the Saxon barons, and installing Norman nobles in their place, he radically changed the manner of government of England, and set it on the path to become a premier European power. The Saxon kings had never really centralized government, established control over all of the dominions of Britain, or formalized systems of taxation and law. Instead each Saxon noble governed relatively autonomously, with little interference or oversight from the King.

The French system of government, inherited by the Romans, was far more formal and centralized, and it was this organizational genius, combined with the energy and industry of the Viking race that had made Normandy a great nation. It was this legacy of energy and organization that William the Conqueror passed on to the reluctant Anglo-Saxon race when he conquered at Senlac, and radically changed the course of English history.

William at the Battle of Hastings

He was the only son of "Robert the Devil", Duke of Normandy, and his commoner mistress, Arletta. Robert however, recognized him as a son, made him his heir, and required his barons to do homage to him. As long as Robert lived, there were no rebellions, but when he died on a pilgrimage to the holy land while William was still a boy, several other claimants to the throne arose, and for a decade Normandy was in a state of near anarchy.

Several of William's guardians were killed and he himself escaped assassination by only a hair. William finally took refuge at the court of Henry I of France, whom both his father and grandfather had served with great distinction. By the time he was nineteen however, he took matters into his own hands, led an army into Normandy and resoundingly defeated the Rebel Barons, much to the delight of the common folk of

Normandy, with whom he was very popular. His troubles were not yet over however. Rebellions continued and eventually even his old patron, Henry I turned against him. But in spite of all obstacles, William prevailed in every battle and gained a great reputation for himself.

In 1053 William married Matilda of Flanders against the recommendation of Rome. Their marriage was notably faithful and happy, and produced ten children. To make amends with the church the couple built cathedrals, schools, and abbeys and donated generously. William was at most times deferential to the interests of the church; his brother Odo was a bishop, and many of the ministers of his government, both in Normandy and England, were churchmen.

William's claim the crown of England was based on the fact that the mother of Edward the Confessor, the last Saxon king of England, was a close cousin. In 1051 William visited England, and it is said at this time that Edward, having no heir himself, named William as his successor.

The choice was a very unpopular one in England, and the Saxon barons elected Harold, son of Godwine, the greatest of the Saxon earls. Harold was not of the royal line however, and had no better claim than William. To complicate matters further, in 1064 Harold was shipwrecked off the coast of Normandy and forced to promise support for William's claim. When Edward the Confessor died in 1066, William prepared a fleet for an invasion, and after a long delay, prevailed over the Saxons at the hard-fought, Battle of Hastings.

Immediately after assuming power, William made sweeping changes to the government of England. Nobles that fully submitted to him were allowed to retain a portion of their power, but rebels were swiftly dealt with, killed or exiled from England, and all of their land confiscated.

He was a heavy-handed ruler, but fair and just; unloved but respected. He had the support of the church and he reformed both laws and taxation to better serve most of the population. He reigned in England for over twenty years after the conquest, and by the end of his reign had thoroughly transformed the government. The greatest conflicts of his later years involved domestic disputes and rebellions led by his eldest son, Robert III, rather than insurrections from unrelated nobles. He was killed by injuries received when he fell of a horse during a siege in France.

 Just over two weeks before the Battle of Hastings in October 1066, William had invaded England, claiming his right to the English throne. In 1051, William is believed to have visited England and met with his cousin Edward the Confessor, the childless English king. According to Norman historians, Edward promised to make William his heir. On his deathbed, however, Edward granted the kingdom to Harold Godwineson (or Godwinson), head of the leading noble family in England and more powerful than the king himself. In January 1066, King Edward died, and Harold Godwineson was proclaimed King Harold II. William immediately disputed his claim.

Battle of Hastings – October 14, 1066

On September 28, 1066, William landed in England at Pevensey, on Britain's southeast coast, with thousands of troops and cavalry. Seizing Pevensey, he then marched to Hastings, where he paused to organize his forces. On October 13, Harold arrived near

Hastings with his army, and the next day, October 14, William led his forces out to battle, which ended in a decisive victory against Harold's men. Harold was killed–shot in the eye with an arrow, according to legend–and his forces were destroyed

Aftermath

After his victory at the Battle of Hastings, William marched on London and received the city's submission. On Christmas Day of 1066, he was crowned the first Norman king of England, in Westminster Abbey, and the Anglo-Saxon phase of English history came to an end.

French became the language of the king's court and gradually blended with the Anglo-Saxon tongue to give birth to modern English. Illiterate as were most nobles of his time, William spoke no English when he ascended the throne and failed to master it despite his efforts. Thanks to the Norman invasion, French was spoken in England's courts for centuries and completely transformed the English language, infusing it with many French words. William I proved an effective king of England, and the "Domesday Book," a great census of the lands and people of England, was among his notable achievements.

Upon the death of William I in 1087, his son, William Rufus

(c.1056-1100), became William II, the second Norman king of England.

Chapter Seven

Back to England After 1066

Sir Reynald I De Gracci (Grey), 1st Baron Gracci of Water Eaton, Norman Knight *son of John I De Grai (Grey), Count of Croix (Croy), Norman Knight -* **Water Eaton, Buckinghamshire, England**

When Sir Reynald I De Gracci (Grey), 1st Baron Gracci of Water Eaton, Norman Knight was born in 1060 in Water Eaton,

De Grai's (Grey) Greystone Castle

Buckinghamshire, his father, John, was 27 and his mother, Adeliza, was 23. He married Lady Joan Ponte Del Arche Baroness Gracci Grey and they had two children together. He then had one son with Adelise FitzOsborne de Peverel. He died in 1097 in Water Eaton, Buckinghamshire, at the age of 37.

De Grey is said to be a descendant of the Norman knight Anchetil de Greye who accompanied William the Conqueror during the conquest of England.

Sir Henry I De Grey, Baron Grey of Water Eaton *son of Sir Reynald I De Gracci (Grey), 1st Baron Gracci of Water Eaton, Norman Knight* - **Water Eaton, Buckinghamshire, England**

Grey Ruthin Castle

When Sir Henry I De Grey, Baron Grey of Water Eaton was born in 1085 in Water Eaton, Buckinghamshire, his father, Sir Reynald, was 25 and his mother, Lady Joan, was 23. He married Annaliese FitzBerne in 1109 in Cornwell, Oxfordshire. They had two children during their marriage. He died in 1140 in Henley On Thames, Oxfordshire, at the age of 55

Sir Henry was the son of Richard de Grey and great-grandson of Anchetil de Greye of Rotherfield Greys, one of the companions of William the Conqueror. Sir Henry was the progenitor of the considerable number of noble houses bearing the name Grey or Gray.

Spread the Nobility
Sir Henry's descendants in the direct male line went on to be ennobled with no less than eighteen peerages, including eleven substantive baronies, a viscountcy, three earldoms (Kent, Tankerville and Grey), a marquessate and two dukedoms.

Sir Henry's descendants through the female line are countless but include the Barons Audley, Barons Revelstoke, Barons Northbrook, Barons Howick, Barons Dacre, Barons Willoughby de Eresby, Earl of Lindsey, the Earls of Malmesbury, Earls of Westmoreland, Earls of Essex, Earls of Durham, Earls of Cromer, Earls of Elgin, Earls of Bridgewater, the Earls of Ashburnham, the Marquesses of Lindsey and the Dukes of Somerset and Ancaster.

92

Sir Lord Richard of Rotherfield Grey *son of Sir Henry I De Grey, Baron Grey of Water Eaton* - **Rotherfield Greys Castle, Henley on Thames, Oxfordshire, England**
Lord Richard Codnor De Grey was born in 1110 the child of Sir

Rotherfield Grey Manor

Anchitel Turgis de and Lady Annaliese. He married Lady Mabilla in 1129 in Oxfordshire. They had eight children in 24 years. His son William became a monk.

Mabilla was born about 1112 in Oxfordshire, England and died at Rotherfield Grey. He died in 1130 in Henley On Thames, Oxfordshire.

Sir Anchitel De Grey, Norman Knight *son of Sir Lord Richard of Rotherfield Grey* - **Rotherfield Greys Castle, Oxfordshire, England**

Rotherfield Greys Castle

Sir Anchitel De Grey, Norman Knight was born about 1135. He married Lady Eva De Redvers in 1155 in Chipping Norton, Oxfordshire. They had 13 children during their marriage. He died about 1160, in Essex, at the age of 25

Anchetil de Greye is listed as one of William the Conqueror's knights sailing to England in 1066 from Notre Dame Church in Dives-sur-Mer "de Grei" and "Anketil") is specifically named in the Domesday Book of 1086.

He was the great-grandfather of John de Grey, Bishop of Norwich, and probably also of Henry de Grey, and the great-great-grandfather of Walter de Grey, Archbishop of York and Lord Chancellor of England. He is regarded as the ancestor of the noble House of Grey.

The principal estate granted to Anchetil de Greye in England was *Redrefield* (subsequently Rotherfield Greys) and the manor house, Greys Court now in South Oxfordshire. Anchetil was also the mesne lord of Standlake now in West Oxfordshire.

94

Sir John De Grey, Earl of Essex *son of Sir Anchitel De Grey, Norman Knight* - **Whitney Castle, Oxfordshire, England**

Grey's Court

When Sir John De Grey, Earl of Essex was born about 1160, in Cornwell, Oxfordshire, his father, Sir Anchitel, was 25 and his mother, Lady Eva, was 21. He married Lady Elena Clare and they had 10 children together. He then married Isabel Bassett in 1175.

He died about 1192, at Witney Castle in Oxfordshire.

Whitney Castle - The castle is recorded as having been captured and burnt in 1401. There is no trace of a castle on the banks of the river Wye today but tradition asserts that beneath the river which changed its course in the year 1730, are still to be seen masses of masonry. The castle was the seat of a most ancient family and flourished for some 500 years, yielding in nearly every generation one or more members of eminence.

Sir Henry De Grey, Earl of Essex *son of Sir John De Grey, Earl of Essex* - **Codnor, Derbyshire, England**

Codnor Castle

When Sir Henry De Grey, Earl of Essex was born in 1176 in Essex, his father, Sir, was 16 and his mother, Lady, was 16. He married Lady Isolda De Bardolf, Countess of Essex in 1180. They had 22 children during their marriage. He died in 1219 in Codnor, Derbyshire, at the age of 43.

In around the year 1200 the manor of Codnor became the property of Henry De Grey through his marriage to Isolda Bardolf, and it was Henry who started the construction of a new and much stronger stone castle that would be the seat of the Grey's of Codnor for around 300 years.

Henry De Grey was a distinguished Baron and had served King Richard I of England abroad on crusade. A French genealogist has traced the Grey linage back to Rollo; he was Chamberlain to Rollo Duke of Normandy. Rollo was given the castle and manor of Croy in Picardy and he took the surname Croy, this later changed to Grey.

On the roll list from the battle of Hastings is listed Gilbert De

Grey from the same family. Henry was a very wealthy and powerful Baron holding lands in Thurrock Essex and lands in Derbyshire. Henry's brother Walter De Grey was also very successful and very influential. Walter was Archbishop of York from 1215 to 1255, and he was present at the signing of Magna Charta with King John and all of the most powerful Barons in England in 1215. Walter De Grey was one of the longest ever standing Archbishop's of York, today you can see his funeral effigy and tomb at York Minster.

Sir Nicholas de Moeles Lord of Cadebury and Saperton, Seneschal of Gascony, Sheriff of Kent, York, Southampton,

Hampshire and Devon; *son of Sir Henry De Grey, Earl of Essex* - **Codnor Castle, Derbyshire, England**

When Sir Nicholas de Moeles Lord of Cadebury and Saperton, Seneschal of Gascony, Sheriff of Kent, York, Southampton, Hampshire and Devon; was born in 1195 his father, Sir, was 19 and his mother, Lady, was 27. He was married four times and had 11 sons and 16 daughters. He died in 1264 in Henley On Thames, Oxfordshire, at the age of 69.

In 1230 Nicholas was granted the Royal Manors of Kingskerswell and Diptford in Devon. Nicholas was Constable of Castle Dover and Lord Warden of the Cinque Ports by 1258.

About 1264 Nicholas De Moels served as the Sheriff of Kent, York, Southampton, his honors extending to the positions of Sheriff of Hampshire and Devon; and Constable of Pembroke, Haverfordwest, Cilgerran, Tenby, Rochester, Canterbury, Winchester and Castle Corfe.

Roger Baron Moleyns Moleyneux Sir of Kings Carswell

Carswell Manor

Manor,Devon de Moels *son of Sir Nicholas de Moeles Lord of Cadebury and Saperton, Seneschal of Gascony, Sheriff of Kent, York, Southampton, Hampshire and Devon; -* **Kings Carswell Manor, Devon, England**

Roger Baron Moleyns Moleyneux Sir of Kings Carswell Manor,Devon de Moels was born in 1233 in Devon, annd his father, Sir Nicholas, was 38 and his mother, Hawise, was 33. He married Lady Alice of Kings Carwell de Preaux/Prouz in 1268 in Somerset. They had 16 children during their marriage. He died on January 17, 1295, in Wincanton, Somerset, at the age of 62.

Sir Roger de Moels/Mules *son of Roger Baron Moleyns Moleyneux Sir of Kings Carswell Manor,Devon de Moels -* **Lustleigh, Devon, Cornwall, England**

When Sir Roger de Moels/Mules was born in 1282 in Lustleigh, Devon, his father, Roger, was 49 and his mother, Lady Alice, was 32. He married Alice Prouse in 1307 in Cornwall. They had 13 children during their marriage. He died in December 1323 in Newton Abbot, Devon, at the age of 41.

He was the third Baron Moles. The title "Baron Moles" was created on February 6, 1299 when his brother, John de Moels, was summoned to parliament as the first Baron Moels.

Sir John DeMules *son of Sir Roger de Moels/Mules -* **Cornwall, England**

When Sir John DeMules was born in 1308 in Cornwall, his father, Sir, was 26 and his mother, Alice, was 22. He married Joan de Lovel, daughter of Richard Lovel of Castle Cary, Somerset. in 1327 in her home town of Somerset. They had four children in 44 years.
He died on August 21, 1337, in Hertfordshire.

James de Meules *son of Sir John DeMules* - **Cornwall, England**

James The Just

James de Meules was born in 1366 in Cornwall. He has one child with Margaret De Mules and one child with Margaret. He died in 1396 in Cornwall, at the age of 30.

Margaret Mulys *daughter of James de Meules* - **Cornwall, England**

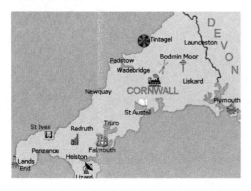

Margaret Mulys was born in 1380 in Cornwall, the child of James and Margaret . She married John Upton in 1400. They had two children during their marriage. She died as a young mother in 1404 in Cornwall, at the age of 24.

Thomas Upton *son of Margaret Mulys* - **Cornwall, England**

Upton Manor House

When Thomas Upton was born in 1416 in Treloish, Cornwall, his father, John, was 37. He married Joanna Trelawny in 1432 in Cornwall. They had two children during their marriage. He died in 1470 in Cornwall, at the age of 54. *His daughter Isabel married John Beckett of Cartthither. This is the family line we will follow to Plymoth Rock and beyond.*

Isabel Upton Beckett *daughter of Thomas Upton* - **Cornwall, England**

When Isabel Upton Beckett was born in 1457 in Cornwall, her father, Thomas, was 41 and her mother, Joanna, was 37. She married John Beckett in 1484 in Cornwall. They had one child during their marriage. She died as a young mother in 1485 in Cornwall, at the age of 28.

John Beckett II *son of Isabel Upton Beckett* - **Cornwall, England**

John Beckett was born in 1482 in Cornwall, the child of John and Isabel. He had one son and one daughter with Joane Totwell. He died in Cornwall.

John is listed in the "Complete Record from the Earliest Times of the Knights of England."

George Beckett *son of John Beckett II* - **Colchester, Essex, England**

St James Church, Colchester

When George Beckett was born in 1500 in Colchester, Essex, his father, John, was 18 and his mother, Joane, was 14. He was married. He died in August 1545 in Suffolk, at the age of 45.

William Beckett *son of George Beckett* - **Juddonham, Suffolk, England**

When William Beckett was born at Haverhill in 1523 his father, George, was 23 and his mother, Emma, was 18. He married Ann Leigh in 1559 in Suffolk. They had one child during their marriage.

William died on November 17, 1563 in Haverhill at the age of 40 and was buried from St Gregory by St Paul in London.

St Gregory's by St Paul's was a parish church in the Castle Baynard ward of the City of London. It was destroyed in the Great Fire of London in 1666 and not replaced. It was built against the walls of St Paul's Cathedral.

Sylvester Beckett *son of William Beckett* - **Juddonham, Suffolk, England**

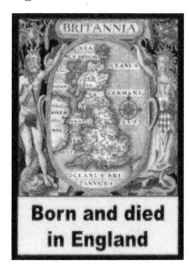

Born and died in England

Sylvester Beckett was born in 1560 in Suffolk, the child of William and Ann. He married Elizabeth Hill of Juddonham in 1582 at Suffolk. They had one daughter, Mary, during their marriage. Sylvester died in 1590 in Worcester, Worcestershire, at the age of 30.

Father of Mary Becket "Mayflower Compact" Soule.

Mary Beckett *daughter of Sylvester Beckett* - **London, England**

Mary Beckett was born on January 17, 1590, in St. Botolphs, London the child of Sylvester and Elizabeth. She married George

"Mayflower Compact" Soule on March 29, 1623, in Duxbury, Massachusetts. They had, by some reports, 13 children during their marriage. She died in December 16, 1676 in Duxbury, Massachusetts, having lived a long life of 86 years.

She migrated to America aboard the "Anne" in 1623 and became the wife of George Soule

The passenger ship "Anne" arrived in Plymouth in July 1623 accompanied by the "Little James," bringing new settlers along with many wives and children who had been left behind in Leiden when the Mayflower departed. Mary Beckett was one of the passengers in "Anne."

The Voyage of the "Anne"

In summer of 1623 about 90 passengers embarked in two small ships sailing from London to Plymouth Colony for the purpose of

The "Anne" 1623

providing settlers and other colony support. These were the 140 ton supply ship *Anne* and the smaller, new 44 ton pinnace which had been outfitted for military service.

They were financed by Thomas Weston's investment group, the Merchant Adventurers, also those who financed the *Mayflower* in 1620 and *Fortune* in 1621.

After a three-month voyage, the *Anne* arrived in Plymouth, per Bradford, on July 10, 1623 and the *Little James* a week or ten days later. After this voyage the *Anne* was to return to its regular cargo shipping work and the *Little James* was to remain in the colony for fishing, cargo and military service. The *Anne's* Master was William Peirce and the *Little James* had two young men in charge – Master John Bridges, master mariner, and a novice Captain, Emmanuel Altham, a Merchant Adventurer.

Passenger Composition

Of the 90-odd passengers, there were about 60 men, women and children total in both ships, many being former English Separatist residents of Leiden, Holland, and with about 30 others being part of an independent emigrant group led by John Oldham. This later group had been promised a separate living situation in Plymouth apart from the main settlement.

There are no separate passenger lists for each ship, as those that sailed in these ships were grouped together in records under the *Anne* when the official land division was made in 1623 with assignment of acreage lots by name. But author Charles Banks did identify at least four men, three with families, who were passengers on the *Little James*. These totaled about 14 persons. Additionally, eight wives accompanied their husbands on these

"Little James" and "Anne" sail to the New World

two ships, along with twelve children most brought over by their parents. At least two of whom were Patience and Fear Brewster, daughters of William and Mary Brewster, who had arrived on the Mayflower.

Association with the *Mayflower*

In the contingent on board the *Anne* were about 15 persons associated in some way with *Mayflower* passengers who had come over in 1620. Some joined husbands or future husbands: Hester Cooke, Bridget Fuller, Alice Bradford, Elizabeth Warren and Barbara Standish. Another had been the spouse of a now-deceased Pilgrim – Sarah Priest Cuthbertson.

There were other passengers who arrived and married *Mayflower* passengers after arrival: Fear Brewster/Isaac Allerton, *Mary Becket/George Soule*, Christian Penn/Francis

Eaton & Francis Billington, Experience Mitchell/Jane Cooke, Nicholas Snow/Constance Hopkins, Sarah Warren/John Cooke, Robert Bartlett/Mary Warren. And there were Mary and Sarah Priest, the daughters of the deceased Pilgrim Degory Priest, who had arrived from Leiden and later married Phineas Pratt and John Coombs respectively.

Not All Made the Grade

Bradford states that some of the new settlers were useful persons and became "good members to the body", some being the wives and children of men there already, some since the *Fortune* came over in 1621. But Bradford also related about those unfit for such a hardship settlement: *"And some were so bad, as they were faine to be at charge to send them home again next year."*

And the state of the passengers is relayed in an apologetic letter sent by Robert Cushman, former Leiden agent in London, to Bradford: *"… It greeveth me to see so weake a company sent you, and yet had I not been here they had been weaker…Shuch and shuch came without my constente: but the importunitie of their freinds got promise of our Treasurer in my absence."*

From these statements it can be learned the reason that so many of the first arrivals disappeared from Plymouth after a few years of experiencing that hardship existence. Many of the emigrants on the *Anne* and *Little James* would eventually be sent back to England as unfit for the task of living and working in a harsh colonial environment.

(Mrs) Frances Palmer - Wife of William Palmer who arrived on the *Fortune* in 1621 with his son William. She received one share in the 1623 land division *as "ffrance wife to Wit Palmer." He was a member of 3 shares as "William, ffrances and Willm Pallmer Jnor"*.

Anne Passengers

Anthony Annable – Married Jane Momford in Cambridge 1619. Had 4 acres in 1623 land division (as Anthony Anable) and four shares in the 1627 cattle division for himself, wife and two daughters. Member of the 1626 Purchaser investment group. Died 1674.

Jane Annable (wife) d.1643

Hannah Annable (daughter)

Sarah Annable (daughter)

Edward Bangs – Born c.1591 - 86 in 1677. Per Banks he was of Panfield, Essex, son of John and Jane (Chavis) Bangs. Shipwright by occupation. The 1623 land division lists 4 shares for him under "Bangs." From that it is thought that he may have had a family of wife and two children with him on the *Anne* that are mysteriously missing by the 1627 cattle division as he only drew one share then. It can only be surmised that something happened to them between 1623 and 1627 as he (re)married after 1627. Member of the 1626 Purchaser investment group as "Edward Banges." He was with those chosen to lay out twenty-acre lots in the 1627 division. After 1627 married Lydia Hicks, daughter of Robert and Margaret Hicks, having been fellow passengers with him on the *Anne* in 1623. Died 1677. Three members of his family that may have been with him as counted in the 1623 land division:

(Mrs) ___ Bangs – possibly died before 1627.

(child) Bangs

(child) Bangs

Robert Bartlett – Cooper (barrel maker) by occupation. Believed to be from Devon, born c.1603. May have arrived as a servant. One share in the 1623 land division as "Robt Bartlet." Married c.1629 Mary, daughter of *Mayflower* **passenger Richard**

Warren. She was also passenger on the *Anne*. Died 1676.

Mary Buckett –Mary Beckett, was a single woman in the 1623 land division as 'Marie Buckett." Married prior to 1627 *Mayflower* **passenger George Soule**. In the 1627 Division of the Cattle she is listed as 'Mary Sowle' with husband George and son Zachariah.

Fear Brewster – Daughter of Elder William Brewster coming from Leiden. In the 1623 land division a portion was given to Fear Brewster along with her sister "Pacience Brewster" and Robert Long. Married *Mayflower* **passenger Isaac Allerton** in 1625 as his 2nd wife. She died in 1634.

Patience Brewster – Daughter of Elder William Brewster coming from Leiden. Allotted a portion in the 1623 land division, with her sister Fear and Robert Long. Married Thomas Prence, passenger on the *Fortune* in 1621 and future colony governor.

Thomas Clarke - Son of John and Mary (Morton) Clarke, baptized Stepney (London) c. 1599-1600. Came over as a young, unmarried man and was allotted one share in the 1623 (as Tho. Clarke) and 1627 divisions. Member of the 1626 Purchaser investment group. Married (1) Susanna Ring, daughter of Mary Ring who was the mother of all his children – William, Andrew, John, James, Susanna, and Nathaniel. Died in Plymouth 1697/8.

Christopher Conant – Baptized in East Budleigh, Devon in 1588, son of Richard and Agnes (Charles) Conant. Went to London in 1609 and became freeman in 1616. Lived in the London parish of St. Lawrence Jewry where his brother **Roger Conant, the founder of Salem, Massachusetts**, married. He had one share in the 1623 land division as "Christopher Connant". Not in the 1627 cattle division and may have left with his brother. Living in Massachusetts Bay Colony in 1630. Probably returned to England.

(Mrs) Hester (Mayhieu) Cooke – A Huguenot who lived in Canterbury, England and Leiden. **Wife of *Mayflower* passenger Francis Cooke** married 1603 in Leiden. With family in 1623 land division, 4 shares. 1627 cattle division – "ffrancis and Hester Cooke" – 7 shares.

Jacob Cooke (son)

Jane Cooke (daughter)

Anthony Dix (Dixe) – Mariner by occupation. Received land in 1623 division as "Anthony Dixe" but number of shares received is illegible. Did not share in 1627 cattle division and may have moved to Salem. Name of his wife was Tabitha, who later married later married Nathaniel Pickman (Pitman). Living in Salem in 1636. Lost at sea in 1639.

John Faunce – His ancestry is uncertain. Received one share in both the 1623 division as "John Fance" and 1627 divisions as "John ffance." Member of the 1626 Purchaser investment group. His wife was Patience Morton, daughter of George and Juliana (Carpenter) Morton, passengers on the Little James. Died in Plymouth 1654

(Mrs) Elizabeth Flavell – Wife of Thomas Flavell, who had come over with an unnamed son in the *Fortune* in 1621. Received one share in the 1623 land division as "goodwife Flauell", but the family was not in the 1627 division.

Edmund Flood – Received one share in the 1623 land division, but was not listed in the 1627 cattle division per Stratton. May have died or left the colony.

(Mrs) Bridget (Lee) Fuller – Third wife of **Samuel Fuller,** an English Separatist from Leiden who **was a *Mayflower*** passenger in 1620. She had one share in the 1623 land division as "Brigett Fuller." Samuel Fuller was the colony's physician and surgeon.

Godbert Godbertson (also known as Cuthbert Cuthbertson) – Hat maker from Leiden, Holland. His 2nd wife Sarah, sister of Pilgrim Isaac Allerton, was twice widowed, the last from *Mayflower* **passenger Degory Priest**. Priest died in the winter of 1620/21 and Sarah returned to Leiden where she remarried sometime after Oct. 25 1621. Her two daughters from her Priest marriage, Mary and Sarah, accompanied them on the *Anne*. In 1623 land division as "Cudbart Cudbartsone" with 6 shares. Member of the 1626 Purchaser investment group as "Cutbert Cutbertson." In the 1627 cattle division as "Godber Godberson" with 5 shares. Both he and his wife died in a 1633 epidemic.

Sarah Godbertson (wife) - She died in a 1633 epidemic.

Samuel Godbertson (son) – Also known as Samuel Cuthbertson or shortened to Cuthbert.

Timothy Hatherley – A London Merchant Adventurer and felt-maker of St. Olaves, Southwark, London. Married Alice Collard in Southwark in 1614. He visited Plymouth in 1623 and returned to England. Member of the 1626 Purchaser investment group (Plymouth and London) as "Mr Hatherley." Taxed in Southwark in 1628. He came again as a settler in 1632 on the *William and Mary*. Died 1666.

William Heard – He received on share in the 1623 land division but did not appear in the 1627 cattle division.

Lydia Hicks – Daughter of Robert and Margaret Hicks – she arrived with her mother Margaret on the *Anne*. After 1627 she married Edward Bangs, a fellow *Anne* passenger.[1]

Margaret Hicks (Hix) – (wife of Robert Hicks) – arrived on the *Anne* with her children Samuel and Lydia to join her husband Robert. In 1623 land division had 4 shares as "Robart Hickes his wife & children." He was a member of the 1626 Purchaser investment group as "Robte Hicks." In 1627 division family had 6 shares. (wife of Robert Hicks)

Samuel Hicks – (son of Robert and Margaret)

(Mrs) ____ Hilton (wife of William Hilton) – Hilton arrived on the *Fortune* in 1621, and his family followed on the *Anne* in 1623. She and her children received 3 acres in the 1623 land division as "William Hiltons wife & .2. children" but did not appear in the 1627 cattle division as they had left Plymouth by then.

Mary Hilton (daughter of William Hilton)

William Hilton (jr) (son of William Hilton)

Edward Holman – Banks believed he was from Clapham, Surrey per Stratton. As a single man he received one share in both the 1623 division as "Edw. Holman" and 1627 division as "Edward Holdman." Member of the 1626 Purchaser investment group. His wife Amy was mentioned in a 1644 deed.

Manassah (Manasseh) Kempton – From Berwick-upon-Tweed on the Scottish border. Later resided in Colchester, Essex. He

appears in the 1623 land division under an erroneous name of
"Manasseh" (with John Faunce as "Fance"). Member of the 1626
Purchaser investment group as "Manaseth Kempton." By the
1627 Division of the Cattle he had married Juliana (Carpenter),
widow of George Morton, they all being *Little James* passengers.
She was eldest and one of five daughters of Alexander Carpenter
of Somerset in England and Leiden in Holland. In the 1627
division they appear as "Manases and Julian Kempton" with her
five Morton children. They had no children together. He died
1664/1665.

Robert Long – He was in the 1623 land division sharing three
acres with sisters Fear and Patience Brewster. No shares in 1627
division. No further record and may have died or left the colony.

Experience Mitchell – He was from Duke's Place, a parish in
Aldgate, London, son of Thomas Mitchell of Cambridge, who
was also of Amsterdam and Leiden. He was living in London in
the summer of 1620. In the 1623 land division he is listed with the
8 shares of the George Morton family. Member of the 1626
Purchaser investment group as "Experience Michell." Married (1)
c.1627 **Jane Cooke, daughter** of **Mayflower passenger Francis
Cooke**. In the 1627 cattle division he is listed within the Francis
Cooke family as "Experience Michaell" including his (future)
wife Jane and other Cooke family members. Died before 14 May
1689, date of inventory.

Thomas Morton Junior – Son of Thomas Morton who came on
the *Fortune* in 1621 and nephew of George Morton, passenger on
Little James. In 1623 received one share and in the 1627 division
is listed with the John Howland family as "Thomas Morton
Junor". Probably remained in the colony as received share in 1652
Dartmouth purchase.

(Mrs) Ellen (Elinor) Newton – She was a young widow of age 25
when she emigrated, dying in 1681 at aged 83. Her ancestry and
name of her husband are unknown. It was believed she may have
been related to one or more of the *Anne* passengers as young
women did not travel alone in those times. In 1623 land division
as "Ellen Newton." By the 1627 cattle division she had married
Fortune passenger John Adams and after his death married
Kenelm Winslow, brother of *Mayflower* passenger Edward

Winslow.

John Oldham – Per Banks he was originally from the town of Derby in Derbyshire. Arrived with his family including his sister Lucretia. In the 1623 land division "Mr Ouldom and those joyned with him" received 10 shares covering his family and others of his group, numbering about 10 persons. They had arranged independent emigration privileges with the Pilgrim authorities. In 1636 he was killed in an Indian attack on Block Island.

(Mrs) John Oldham (wife).

Mary Oldham (daughter). Married *Little James* passenger William Bridges.

Lucretia Oldham (sister) – Married Jonathan Brewster, eldest son of Elder William Brewster

(Mrs) Frances Palmer - Wife of William Palmer who arrived on the *Fortune* in 1621 with his son William. She received one share in the 1623 land division as "ffrance wife to Wit Palmer." He was a member of the 1626 Purchaser investment group as "Willm Palmer." In the 1627 division the family had 3 shares as "William, ffrances and Willm Pallmer Jnor". William Palmer died in 1637.

Christian Penn – A female of the John Oldham group but oddly no connection to any other *Anne* passenger is known. She received one share in the 1623 land division and one share in the 1627 division as "Christian Eaton" which indicates **she married** *Mayflower* **passenger Francis Eaton** prior to 1627 as his 3rd wife. They had a daughter Rachell born 1627 so may have married about 1625/6. After Eaton's death in 1633 **she married** *Mayflower* **passenger Francis Billington** in 1634.

Abraham Pierce (or Peirce) – He was named with 2 servants in the 1623 division as "Mr Perces .2. ser:" Member of the 1626 Purchaser investment group as "Abraham Pearse." In the 1627 division he had one share as "Abraham Peirce." Died c.1633.

(name unknown) - servant of A. Pierce (1623)

(name unknown) – servant of A. Pierce (1623)

Joshua Pratt – Per Banks he was a brother of Phineas Pratt who came on the *Sparrow* in 1622 in the employ of Adventurer Thomas Weston with his failed settlement at Wessagusset (now Weymouth). In both the 1623 and 1627 divisions he was listed with 1 share with his brother Phineas (also 1 share) as in 1623 "Josuah and Phineas Prat" and in 1627 as "Joshua and Phinihas Pratt." Member of the 1626 Purchaser investment group as "Josuah Pratt." His brother Phineas was also a Purchaser member. Died c.1656.

Mary Priest (step-daughter of Godbert Godbertson) – **daughter of** *Mayflower* **passenger Degory Priest**. Later married Phineas Pratt, brother of *Anne* passenger Joshua Pratt.

Sarah Priest (step-daughter of Godbert Godbertson) – **daughter of** *Mayflower* **passenger Degory Priest.** Later married John Coombs (Combe).

James Rande (Rand) – Per Banks he was possibly from St. George's parish, Southwark, London. Received one share in 1623 land division (as James Rande) but was not in 1627 cattle division. He either died or left the colony.

Robert Ratcliffe (Rattlife) – He was a native of Cheshire. Received two shares in the 1623 land division as "Robart Rattlife" indicating his wife was with him. He was not in the 1627 cattle division. No further record indicating he either died or left the colony.

(Mrs) ___ Ratcliffe

Nicolas (Nicholas) Snow – Banks believed he was of Hoxton, Middlesex, (London), son of Nicholas Snow. Baptized at St. Leonard's, Shoreditch, London, the parish adjoining St. Mary's Whitechapel where Stephen Hopkins (whose daughter Constance became his wife) was married in 1618. Banks believed the Hopkins family emigration caused Nicholas Snow to follow. But since burial records for St. Leonard's have become available we see that the child baptized 25 January 1599/1600 was buried 3 days later and could not be the husband of Constance Hopkins. He is listed in the 1623 land division as "Nicolas Snow." Member of the 1626 Purchaser investment group. By the 1627 division of cattle **he was married to** *Mayflower* **passenger Constance Hopkins**, daughter of Stephen, listed as "Nickolas" and

Constance Snow with the Stephen Hopkins family.

(Mrs) Alice (Carpenter) Southworth – born about 1591, one of five daughters of Alexander and Priscilla Carpenter of Wrington, co. Somerset in England and later Leiden, Holland. She was the widow of Edward Southworth, who died 1621/22, and her future husband was William Bradford. She married Governor William Bradford in Plymouth on August 14, 1623, a few weeks after arriving on the ship *Anne*. Her sister Julian was on the accompanying ship *Little James* with husband George Morton and her children. In the 1623 Land Division she is listed as "Allice Bradford" and in the 1627 Division of the Cattle as "Alles Bradford" with her children William Bradford Junior and Mercy Bradford. Sometime after 1627 her sons with Edward Southworth, Constant (born c. 1614) and Thomas (born c. 1617) joined her at Plymouth.

Francis Sprague – Banks states his ancestry is unknown, although it was probable he was married and past middle age when he emigrated. His wife may have been deceased and both females with him may have been his daughters. He had three shares in the 1623 land division as "Francis Spragge" and was in the 1627 cattle division (as "ffrancis, Anna and Mercye Sprage") with Anna and Mercy Sprague, Anna's status unknown whether wife or daughter, Mercy being a daughter. He was a member of the 1626 Purchaser Investment group. Died c.1670.

Anna Sprague (wife or daughter – status unknown)

Mercy Sprague (daughter)

Thomas Tilden – Per Banks probably from Tenterden, Kent, where he was baptized in 1593, younger brother of Nathaniel Tilden who emigrated in 1635. Received three shares in the 1623 land division, indicating he was accompanied by a wife and child.

(Mrs) _____ Tilden

(child) Tilden

Stephen Tracey (Tracy) – He was a mariner by occupation. He was baptized in Great Yarmouth, Norfolk in 1596, son of Stephen and Agnes (Erdley) Tracy. Occupation of say(cloth)-weaver in Leiden where he married Tryphosa Lee in 1621. He came over directly from Leiden. He had 3 acres in the 1623 land division as "Steph: Tracy" meaning wife and daughter Sarah must have also been on the *Anne*, although Stratton states may have arrived by 1625. Member of the 1626 Purchaser investment group as "Steeven Tracy." He had four shares in the 1627 division for himself and wife "Triphosa", and daughters Sarah and "Rebecka." He returned to England on a business trip cir. 1654 and died in London after March, 1655. He prepared a legal document to dispose of his estate in Duxbury, Plymouth, Massachusetts to his wife and children who remained in New England.

Tryphosa Tracy (wife)

Sarah Tracy (daughter)

Ralph Wallen – Arrived with his wife Joyce. In 1623 land division as "Ralfe Walen" with unknown shares. Member of the 1626 Purchaser investment group as "Raph Wallen." Named in the 1627 cattle division with wife Joyce. Died c.1643.

Joyce Wallen (wife)

(Mrs) Elizabeth Warren – **Wife of *Mayflower* passenger Richard Warren**. Came over with 5 daughters. In 1623 land division he is listed as "Richard Waren" with 5 shares. In the 1627 cattle division the family is listed with 9 shares – parents and 7 children. Richard Warren died in 1628. After her husband's death, she became an after-the-fact member of the 1626 Purchaser investment group as "Elizabeth Warren, widow." She died in 1673, aged ninety years.

Abigail Warren (daughter) – later married Anthony Snow.

Ann (Anna) Warren (daughter) – later married Thomas Little.

Elizabeth Warren (jr) (daughter) – later married Richard Church.

Mary Warren (daughter) – later married Robert Bartlett, *Anne* passenger.

Sarah Warren (daughter) – later **married *Mayflower* passenger John Cooke**.

Barbara (unknown) – Future (2nd) **wife of *Mayflower* passenger Myles Standish**. Married sometime after arrival before 1627 and by whom he had all his known children. She did appear in the

1623 land division as "Mrs Standish." The 5-member family appears in the 1627 division with three sons and with the Winslow and White families. Standish was Plymouth Colony's chief military officer. Member of the 1626 Purchasers investment group as "Capt Miles Standish." Myles Standish died in 1656. His wife died sometime after that year.

Priscilla and John Alden

Little James Passengers

William Bridges – Possible brother or kinsman of John Bridges, Master of Little James. He was a son-in-law of John Oldham, married to his daughter Mary Oldham. In later years he stated in a petition he came over with his father-in-law in 1623. In the 1623 land division, his name does not appear but he may have been represented by John Oldham's 10 shares. Per Stratton he resided in the Bay Colony.

Edward Burcher – He was probably of Southwark St. Saviour parish, London. He was beyond middle life on this voyage as the *Little James* captain wrote about he and his wife: "Father Birrtcher and his wife wear as hartey as the youngest in the ship." He received two shares in the 1623 land division for himself and his wife. He was not in the 1627 cattle division.

(Mrs) ___ Burcher

John Jenney – He was a cooper (barrel maker) by occupation. Leiden records call him a "brewer's man" of Norwich, Norfolk. He was ship's cooper on Little James. Arrived on the *Little James* with wife Sarah and children Samuel, Abigail, and Sarah. Son Samuel was born on the ship. Captain Altham wrote on September 7, 1623 that *"Good wife Jennings was brought abed of a son aboard our ship." And: "was delivered of a child in the Ship a month before we cam a shore and both are well yet, God be praised."* In the 1623 land division he is "John Jenings" with 5 shares. He was a member of the 1626 Purchaser investment group as "Mr John Jenney". In the 1627 cattle division he is "John Jene" with 5 members of his family and 6 members of the Hicks (Hickes) family listed with him in the 12th lot. Died after c.1643.

Sarah Jenney (wife) – She was Sarah Carey of Monk Soham,

Suffolk. Married 1613 in Leiden.

Abigail Jenney (daughter)

Samuel Jenney (son – born on board Little James)

Sarah Jenney (daughter)

George Morton – historically famous to Plymouth Colony by being revealed as the author (possibly with William Bradford and Edward Winslow) of Mourt's Relations, a manuscript of life and times from the earliest colony days, published in England in 1622. Morton was of York or Nottinghamshire in the north of England. He married Juliann Carpenter, then about twenty-five, in Leiden on July 22, 1612. She was the eldest of the five daughters of Alexander Carpenter of Wrington, co. Somerset in England and of Leiden in Holland.

Juliann's sister Alice was on the ship accompanying the *Anne*, the little James. She came as a widow but soon **married *Mayflower* passenger Governor Bradford**. The Thomas Morton who came over on the Fortune in 1621 may have been his brother with the Thomas Morton Jr. who came on the Ann possibly being Thomas's son and George's nephew. Morton died in June 1624, about a year after arriving in Plymouth. In the 1627 Division of the Cattle, the Morton children are listed with his wife Juliann now listed under her second husband's surname as "Julian Kempton" (Stratton).

Juliann * (Carpenter) Morton –She was baptized in March 1584 at St. James church in Bath, co. Somerset. After her husband's death in 1624 she married "Manasseh" Kempton. In the 1627 Division of the Cattle she and her second husband are listed along with the five Morton children. She died in Plymouth, February 19, 1664.

Note: other writers report her name as Juliana (author Stratton) or Julian (author Banks). Johnson reports her name in the 1627 Division of the Cattle as "Juliana Kempton."

Nathaniel Morton (age 10). He later became Secretary (Clerk) of the Plymouth General Court. He married Lydia Cooper, sister of John Cooper, husband of his aunt Priscilla (Carpenter) Wright Cooper.

Patience Morton (age 8). In the 1630s she married John Faunce, an *Anne* passenger.

John Morton (son) aged 6.

Sarah Morton (age 3). She married William Dennis on December 20, 1644.

Ephraim Morton (infant). He married Ann Cooper, daughter of his aunt Priscilla (Carpenter) Wright Cooper.

About George Soule

George was born in 1590 at Eckington, Worcestershire, England. He came the New World aboard the Mayflower and was a signer of the "Mayflower Compact."

George was orphaned as a young boy when fire destroyed his home in Eckington, England. His brother, Robert Soule, a Salters Company employee, raised him up.

He was 27 years old when the Mayflower arrived at Plymouth. He came as a teacher (servant) to Edward Winslow's children. He latter married Mary Beckett who came to Plymouth aboard the "Anne" in 1623.

Excerpts from; *The English Ancestry and Homes of the Pilgram fathers by Charles Edward Banks 1984.*
He (George Soule) has been identified as son of John Soule of Eckington, Worcester, and probably kinsman to Robert Soule, a wealthy London salter, who died in 1590 also native of Eckington.

The Winslow family lived in the nearby parish of Kempsey, Co. Worcester, and it is probable that this early neighborhood association explains the apprenticeship of George Soule to Plymouth colony's Governor Winslow. It is supposed that George Soule was in London when he joined Winslow on the voyage. Droitwich, the family home of the Winslow's at that time, was a salt mining place connected in a business way with the Salters' Company of London in trade, and thus the Winslow-Soule association.

Indians taken prisoner during the Pequot War

The name of Mary (Bucket) Beckett, his wife, who came in the Anne, should be looked for in the parish of St. Botolph, Aldersgate, London. George Soule and Mary were married in Plymouth.

George Soule, Miles Standish and John Alden laid out the first town, Duxbury, and are buried there.

In 1637, Soule volunteered to serve during the Pequot War. The Pequot War was an armed conflict in 1634-1638 between the Pequot tribe against an alliance of the Massachusetts Bay and Plymouth colonies with Native American allies (the Narragansett and Mohegan tribes). The result was the elimination of the Pequot as a viable entity in what is present-day Southern New England. Most of the Pequot people, warriors or otherwise, were killed by the colonists and their allies, or captured and sold into slavery in Bermuda. Other survivors were dispersed.

John Soule *son of Mary Beckett Soule and George Soule* –
Plymouth,

When John Soule was born in 1632 in Plymouth, Massachusetts, his father, George, was 37 and his mother, Mary, was 42. He married Rebecca Simmons and they had 15 children together. She died and he then married Esther Nash in 1678 in Massachusetts.

Esther was the widow of Samuel Sampson and her four children; two daughters, Elizabeth and Mary Sampson Howland and two sons, Samuel and Ichahod, when she married John.

Samuel Sampson Sr and John Soule had been good friends and after Samuel was killed in the King Philip's War, John was named co-executor of his estate.

His father George's will dated Aug, 11, 1677 reads: *"My eldest son who hath in my extreme old age and weakness ben tender and careful of mee and very helpful to mee and likely to be, while it shall please God to continue my life heer; therefore I will give and bequeath unto my said son John Soule all the remainder of my housing whatsoever. My son John Soule to be my sole executor."*

John died on November 14, 1707, in Duxbury, Massachusetts, at 75 years of age and was buried in the Myles Standish Burying Grounds in Duxbury.

Children of George Soule and Mary Beckett

1. **Zachariah** was born by May 1627 and died in Duxbury before 11 December 1663. He married Margaret _____ by 1663, No known children have been identified and the widow is believed to have remarried and moved from Duxbury.

   He was a combatant in the French & Indian War; on the latter date his estate was inventoried at Duxbury, Mass. by John Alden and Constant Southworth with the estate falling to his brother John after settlement.

2. **John** was born about 1632 and died in Duxbury before 14 November 1707. He was married twice:

   1) about 1656 Rebecca Simonson, daughter of Moses Simonson, by whom he had nine known children. She died between 1675 and 1678.

   2) about 1679 Esther (Delano) Samson, daughter of Philip Delano and widow of Samuel Samson, by whom he had three children.

3. **Nathaniel** was born between 1634 and 1646 and died in Dartmouth before 12 October 1699. He married Rose Thorn by 1680 and had five children. Nathaniel may have caused the most colony trouble of any of his siblings. On 5 March 1667/8, he made an appearance in Plymouth court to "answer for his abusing of Mr. John Holmes, teacher of the church of Christ at Duxbury, by many false, scandalous and opprobrious speeches." He was sentenced to make a public apology for his actions, find sureties for future good behavior and to sit in the stocks, with the stock sentence remitted.

4. His father George and brother John had to pay surety for Nathaniel's good behavior with he being bound for

monies and to pay a fine. Three years later, on 5 June 1671, he was fined for "telling several lies which tended greatly to the hurt of the Colony in reference to some particulars about the Indians." And then on 1 March 1674/5 he was sentenced to be whipped for "lying with an Indian woman," and had to pay a fine in the form of bushels of corn to the Indian woman towards the keeping of her child.

5. **George** was born about 1639 and died in Dartmouth before 22 June 1704 at 34 years of age. He married by 1671 Deborah _____ and had eight children. She died in Dartmouth on February, 10 1709.

6. **Susanna** was born about 1640 and died in North Kingstowne, Rhode Island. She married Francis West Sr. by 1660 and had nine children. He died January 2, 1695/96.

7. **Mary** was born about 1642 and died in Plymouth after 1720. She married John Peterson by 1665 and had nine children. He died between 29 April 1718 and 26 March 1720, probably in Plymouth.

Elizabeth was born about 1644 and died after 1667. She married Francis Walker by 23 July 1668 and had one child. He died in probably Middleboro about 1701. Elizabeth, like her brother Nathaniel, also had her share of problems with the Plymouth Court. On 3 March 1662/3, the Court fined Elizabeth and Nathaniel Church for committing fornication. Elizabeth then in turn sued Nathaniel Church "for committing an act of fornication with her... and then denying to marry her." The jury awarded her damages plus court costs. On 2 July 1667 Elizabeth was sentenced to be whipped at the post "for committing fornication the second time." And although the man with whom she committed the act was not named.

8. Elizabeth did marry Francis Walker on July 23, 1667 at Woodbridge, New Jersey. They had four children together. She died. circa 1700 and he; died circa 1702 – both at Woodbridge, New Jersey.

9. **Patience** was born about 1646 and died on 11 March 1705/6 in Middleboro. She married John Haskell in January 1666/7 in Middleboro and had eight children. He died on 15 May 1706 in Middleboro.

10. **Benjamin** was born by about 1652 and died unmarried during King Philip's War on 26 March 1676.

George Soule's signature

Follow the "Olive Branch" out of the Garden of Eden

Start the Journey again; this time following George and Mary Soule's 3rd great granddaughter Olive (daughter of Asaph) Soule's, trip from the Garden of Eden to New England.

This branch took a completely different route and a few more generations to make the journey. Instead of coming to the British Isles and Ireland sometime before 600 BC as did the other branch, this branch flowed throughout Asia, Greece and Greek Mythology (some calling themselves gods). They were the Trojans who established the roots of European royalty around 1,000 BC.

They exited out of Asia into Europe (Germany) around the beginning of the Christian Era moving into France about a thousand years later. It was in France, Normandy, that the two branches joined together under our relative William the Conqueror and defeated England at the Battle of Hastings in 1066.

Six hundred years later two of our decedents, George Soule and Mary Beckett, left the comforts of then modern day England to venture thousands of miles across the sea to establish themselves in a primitive wilderness.

Chapter Eight

Olive Soule's Branch Begins Their Journey

Shem ben Noah - *son of Noah Ben Lamech* - **East Eden**

Shem ben Noah has four children with Sedeqetelebab Bint Eliakim and five children with Sedeqetelebab. He had eight brothers.

Genesis 11:10 records that Shem was 100 years old at the birth of his son Arphaxad, two years after the flood; and that he lived for another 500 years after this, making his age at death 600 years

Arphaxad ben Shem, King of Arrapachtis - *son of Shem ben Noah* - **Babylon**

Arphaxad ben Shem, King of Arrapachtis had four sons with Rasueja Rasueya bint Shushan. He had four brothers.

Arpachshad, alternatively spelled Arphaxad or Arphacsad was one of the five sons of Shem, the eldest son of Noah (*Genesis* 10:22, 24; 11:10-13; *1 Chron.*

129

1:17-18). Arpachshad's brothers were Elam, Asshur, Lud and Aram; he is an ancestor of Abraham. He is said by Gen. 11:10 to have been born two years after the Flood, when Shem was 100.

Arpachshad's son is called Shelah, except in the Septuagint, where his son is Cainan, Shelah being Arpachshad's grandson. Cainan is also identified as Arpachshad's son in Luke 3:36 and Jubilees 8:1. The Book of Jubilees additionally identifies Arpachshad's wife as *Rasu'aya*, the daughter of *Susan*, who was the son (or daughter in some versions) of Shem's older son Elam. (Arpachshad's mother is named in this source as *Sedeqetelebab*.

Mesopotamia Roots Set In Europe

Mesopotamia has been identified as having "inspired some of the most important developments in human history including the invention of the wheel, the planting of the first cereal crops and the development of cursive script, mathematics, astronomy and agriculture.

Mesopotamia is widely considered to be one of the cradles of

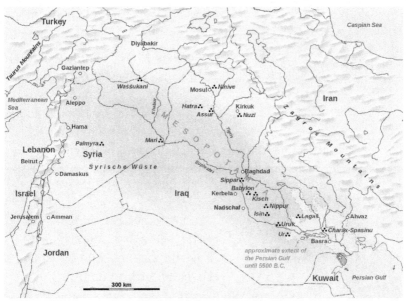

Ancient Mesopotamia

civilization in the; Western world, Bronze Age Mesopotamia, Babylonian, and Assyrian empires. All now known as Iraq.

DNA Tests Prove Long Ago Connections

Studies have reported that most Irish and Britons are descendants of farmers who left modern day Iraq and Syria thousands of years ago. Genetic researchers say they have found compelling evidence that four out of five (80% of) white Europeans can trace their roots to the Near East. In another study, scientists analyzed DNA from the 8,000-year-old remains of early farmers found at an ancient graveyard in Germany.

They compared the genetic signatures to those of modern populations and found similarities with the DNA of people living in today's Turkey and Iraq.

Cainain SEMITE ben Arphaxad - *son of Arphaxad ben Shem, King of Arrapachtis* – **Babylon**

Cainain SEMITE ben Arphaxad was born in Lebanon. He had five sons with Rasueja Bint Elam. He also married Melka bint Madai Medai Madian in Ur, Languedoc-Roussillon, France. He died in 1904 BC.

Cainan is sometimes called Shelah, is identified as Arpachshad's son in Luke 3:36 and Jubilees 8:1. The Book of Jubilees additionally identifies Arpachshad's wife as *Rasu'aya*, the daughter of *Susan*, who was the son of Shem's older son Elam.

Lost Ten Tribes of Israel

The Children of Israel arrived in Europe and the British Isles at various times during ancient history via differing migration patterns. The earliest records of the arrival of these Israelis and Egyptians occurred in Ireland at the time of the Exodus over 3,000 years ago.

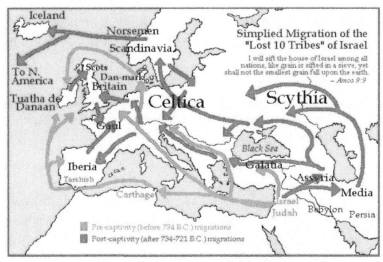

Migration Across the World

There's strong evidence to support the theory that Britain is mainly occupied today by descendants of the original Ten Lost Tribes of Israel. Moreover, is suggested that Henry VIII held this same belief when he established the Church of England after his excommunication from the Roman Catholic Church.

The chart above displays the routes that began in Israel, first went to Troy, then to Russia, Ukraine, then to Scandanavia, Germany, France before ending in the Britain and America.

Shelah Sale Salah CHALDEA Ben Arphaxad - *son of Cainain SEMITE ben Arphaxad* - **Jerusalem, Israel**

Sala, a/k/a Sale, Shelah, Salah, was King of Babalyon and Chaldea. King of BABYLON; of CHALDEA; eponym of the HEBREWS; `Be high gift from God'; poss. aka Ibiranu I (King) of UGARIT; aka Hud (4th Prophet of ISLAM); (according to the Koran, by Hud's time man had forgotten the lesson of the Great Flood, so Allah sent a Great Drought with few survivors).

Shelah Sale Salah CHALDEA Ben Arphaxad was born in Israel. He married Muak Muak bint Kesed and they had three children together. He then had one son with Rasueja Rasueya bint Shushan. In 1874 BC he died in Jerusalem, Israel.

Eber ('Aybar) ben Shelah King of BABYLON - *son of Shelah Sale Salah CHALDEA Ben Arphaxad* – **Canaan, Israel**

Eber ('Aybar) Ibn Shelah King of BABYLON had one son with Semite Muak. He then married Azurad bint Nebrod and they had 13 children together. He had two brothers.
Eber is an ancestor of the Israelites, according to the "Table of Nations" in Genesis 10-11 and 1 Chronicles 1. He was a great-grandson of Noah's son Shem and the father of Peleg born when Eber was 34 years old, and of Joktan.
He was the son of Shelah a distant ancestor of Abraham.
According to the Hebrew Bible, Eber died at the age of 464 (Genesis 11:14-17) when Jacob was 20. The Hebrew Calendar synchronises this date with 1817 BCE.

Variations: In the Septuagint and in Christian Bibles derived from it, Eber is called Heber and his father is called Sala. His son is called Phaleg, born when Heber was 134 years old, and he had other sons and daughters. Heber lived to an age of 404 years. (Septuagint Genesis 11:14-17)

Saved the "Original Human Language"

In Jewish tradition, Eber, the great-grandson of Shem, refused to help with the building of the Tower of Babel, so his language was not confused when it was abandoned. He and his family alone retained the original human language, Hebrew, a language named after Eber (Heber), also called lingua humana in Latin. [Genesis 10:21] Also to Shem, the father of all the Children of Eber, and the older brother of Japheth, children were born.

In some translations of the New Testament, he is referred to once as Heber ([Luke 3:35] ...the son of Serug, the son of Reu, the son of Peleg, the son of Heber, the son of Salah...); however, he should not be confused with the Heber of the Old Testament (different Hebrew spelling ???), grandson of Asher ([Genesis 46:17] The sons of Asher: Imnah and Ishvah and Ishvi and Beriah and their sister Serah.

Linguistic Association of "Eber", "Heber" and "Hebrew"

In the King James Version (KJV) of the Old Testament, the name "Eber" is used, while in the KJV New Testament, "Heber" is used instead, each referring to the same person. And in both KJV books, the word "Hebrew" refers to the descendants of this person. The confusion between "Eber" and "Heber" lies in transcriptional misunderstandings through ongoing layers of Biblical translation, as well as the differentiated cultural origins of the Old and New Testaments.

The origin of the names for Eber and the Hebrews, as used in European Christian languages, derived from Aramaic as spoken in the Roman province of Judaea and by those Jews who escaped the province's destruction. When Greek-writing Jewish scholars compiled the Septuagint, the adaptations chosen for these names (for whatever reason) were Heber and Hebraios.

These names were adapted through Latin and French before reaching English as "Heber" and "Hebrew", and these names were used in the KJV New Testament.

However, the KJV Old Testament was largely translated not from Greek and Latin sources, but from existing Hebrew texts accessible to scholars at the time, employing a uniquely Anglo-Saxon method of adapting Hebrew words and names. As such, in the Old Testament, "Eber" was used without the H, likely reflecting the common Hebrew dialects used among the Jews of Europe. However, the KJV translators chose to use the New Testament name "Hebrew" (instead of "Ibrite" or "Eberite") as the canonical term for the descendants of Eber in the Old Testament as well, likely to avoid confusing lay readers.

As the King James Version of the Bible became the primary Christian scripture of Great Britain, the association of "Eber" with "Hebrew" in the English-speaking religious world became a permanent phenomenon. Another version: In Jewish tradition,

Oldest known version of the 10 Commandments

Eber, the great-grandson of Shem, refused to help with the building of the Tower of Babel, so his language was not confused when it was abandoned. He and his family alone retained the original human language, Hebrew, a language named after Eber (Heber), also called *lingua humana* in Latin.

135

Hebrew Writings Carved in Stone Found in America

Carving dated to 1,500BC

Near Alberquerque, New Mexico is an acient Israelite Tabernacle site dating back to 1,500 BC. The 80 ton boulder, "Commandments Stone," is dated to the Old Testement period in the Paleo-Hebrew "mother script." It paraphrases the Ten Command – ments: *"I am Yahweh thy God who brought thee out of the land"* and began with *"There shall not be unto them other Gods before Me,"*

Ohio Decalogue Stone and Keystone
In November of 1860, David Wyrick of Newark, Ohio found an inscribed stone in a burial mound about 10 miles south of

Newark. The stone is inscribed on all sides with a condensed version of the Ten Commandments or Decalogue, in a peculiar form of post-Exilic square Hebrew letters. The robed and bearded figure on the front is identified as Moses in letters fanning over his head.

Other Paleo-Hebrew inscriptions have been discovered in the states of Tennessee, Iowa and in Mexico and Brazil

These various inscriptions establish that the Israelites, and perhaps our ancestors, were in America long before the Mayflower pilgrims.

Pelag Phaleg Falikh Peleg of BABYLON - son *of Eber ('Aybar)*
Ibn Shelah King of BABYLON - **Salem, Jerusalem, Palestine**

The Tower of Babel

Pelag Phaleg Falikh Peleg of BABYLON was born and died in Jerusalem, Israel. He married Lomna bint Sinaar in Jerusalem, Israel. They had seven children during their marriage.

Pelag is mentioned in the Hebrew Bible as one of the two sons of Eber, an ancestor of the Israelites, according to the "Table of Nations" in Genesis 10-11 and 1 Chronicles 1. Peleg's son was Reu, born when Peleg was thirty, and he had other sons and daughters. According to the Hebrew Bible, Peleg lived to the age of 239 years. (Genesis 11:1619)

According to Genesis 10:25 and 1 Chronicles 1:19, it was during the time of Peleg that "the earth was divided" – traditionally, this is often assumed to be just before, during, or after the failure of Nimrod's Tower of Babel. The meaning of the earth being divided is usually taken to refer to a patriarchal division of the world, or possibly just the eastern hemisphere, into allotted portions among the three sons of Noah for future occupation, as specifically described in the *Book of Jubilees*, *Biblical Antiquities of Philo*, *Kitab al-Magall*, Flavius Josephus, and numerous other antiquarian and mediaeval sources, even as late as Archbishop Ussher, in his *Annals of the World*.

Reu Rau Lagash - *son of Pelag Phaleg Falikh Peleg of BABYLON-* Ur

Reu Rau Lagash married Ora Bat Ur in Ur, Languedoc-Roussillon, France. They had seven children during their marriage. He had six brothers.

Reu ben Peleg, the Semite, was born 2217 BCE. He married 'Ôrâ bat 'Ûr ben Kesed, daughter of 'Ûr ben Kesed, 2319 B.C. In 1681 A.M., in the thirty-fifth jubilee, in the third week, in the first year; Jubilees 11:1 "... Reu took to himself a wife, and her name was 'Ora." He was per Genesis 11:18 and Luke 3:35, the son of Pelag, and per Jubilees 10:18, his wife Lomna. Also called Ragau.

When Reu had lived 32 years, he became the father of Serug. And after he became the father of Serug, Reu lived 207 years and had other sons and daughters. (Gen 11:20-21)

The City of Ur

Ur is considered to be the city of Ur Kasdim mentioned in the

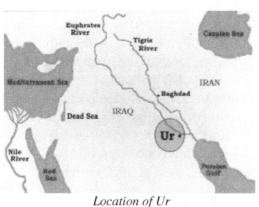

Book of Genesis as the birthplace of the Hebrew and Arab patriarch Abram (Abraham; Aramaic: Oraham, Arabic: Ibrahim), traditionally believed to be some time in the 2nd millennium BC.

Location of Ur

Ur is mentioned four times in the Torah or Old Testament, with the distinction "of the Kasdim/Kasdin"—traditionally rendered in English as "Ur of the Chaldees". The Chaldeans were already settled in the vicinity by around 850 BC, but were not the rulers of

Ur until the late 7th century BC, around 550 BC. The name is found in Genesis 11:28, Genesis 11:31, and Genesis 15:7. In *Nehemiah* 9:7, a single passage mentioning Ur is a paraphrase of *Genesis*. (Nehemiah 9:7)

The *Book of Jubilees* states that Ur was founded in 1688 *Anno Mundi* (year of the world) by 'Ur son of Kesed, presumably the offspring of Arphaxad, adding that in this same year wars began on Earth.

"And 'Ur, the son of Kesed, built the city of 'Ara of the Chaldees, and called its name after his own name and the name of his father." (i.e., *Ur Kasdim*) (Jubilees 11:3).

Serug Sorogh Sargun Sarug Saragh (Saruch King of Ur and Agade) - *son of Reu Rau Lagash* - **Ur,**

Serug Sorogh Sargun Sarug Saragh Saruch King of Ur and Agade was born in Ur, Languedoc-Roussillon, France.

He married Melka Bint KABER, they had 21 children during their marriage. He died in 1951 BC

Jubilees 11:1-2 States that his original name was Seroh, but that it was changed to Serug in the time when Noah's children began to fight wars, and the city of Ur, where Serug lived was built. It says this Serug was the first of the patriarchal line to abandon monotheism and turn to idol worship, teaching sorcery to his son Nahor.

Nahor Ben Serug Ur Agade *son of Serug Sorogh Sargun Sarug Saragh Saruch King of Ur and Agade -* **Ur**

Nahor Ben Serug Ur Agade married Iyaska Jaska ijaska Bint Nestag Chaldees and they had 13 children together. He then had one son with Amthelo Bas Avram Agade. He had nine brothers and seven sisters. In 2003 BC he died in Ur Nahor, Nachor, or Naghor is the son of Serug. In Genesis Chapter 11, Nahor is listed as the son of Serug.

According to some interpretations, he was born and raised in the Sumerian city-state of Ur on the Euphrates River of lower Mesopotamia, about four Millennia ago. He is said to have lived to the age of 148 years old and had a son, Terah at the age of 29. He was also the grandfather of Abraham, Nahor II and Haran, all descendants of Shem

Terah Thara *- son of Nahor Ben Serug Ur Agade -* **Ur,**

Terah Thara married AMTHELO Agade in 1917 BC. They had 15 children during their marriage. He had four brothers.

Terah meaning "wild goat", or "Wanderer, loiterer" is a biblical figure in the Book of Genesis. ,

Terah's son Abram had an encounter with God, who directed him to take the entire family, leave Ur, and move to the land of Canaan. Terah coordinated the journey, intending to go to this new land, but stopped in the city of Haran along the way, where he died at the age of 205.

Abraham Abram Terah - *son of Terah Thara* - **Ur**

Abraham had 17 sons. He had 10 brothers and four sisters.
Abraham is mentioned in both the Old and New Testaments. The
majority of information regarding him is recorded in the book of
Genesis. He had three sons: Abram, Haran, and Nahor. The
family resided in Ur of the Chaldees.

Abraham, had an encounter with God who told him to take the
whole family and leave Ur to go the land of Canaan.
Abraham, sometimes referred to as Abram, was a descendant of
Shem, and he married his half sister Sarai, or Sarah. They left Ur
with his nephew Lot and Lot's family under a divine inspiration
and went to Haran.
Receiving a promise that God would make him a "great nation,"
Abram moved on to Canaan, where he lived as a nomad. Famine
led him to Egypt, but he was driven out for misrepresenting Sarai
as his sister. Again in Canaan, after quarrels between Abram and
Lot and their herdsmen, they separated, Lot remaining near
Sodom and Abram continuing his nomadic life.
He later rescued Lot from the captivity of King Chedorlaomer of
Elam and was blessed by the priest Melchizedek, King of Salem.
Then God promised Abram a son by his wife Sarai, repeated his
earlier promises, and confirmed these by a covenant.

When this covenant was later renewed, the rite of circumcision was established, Abram's name became Abraham, and Sarai's became Sarah. God subsequently repeated his promise of a son by Sarah by means of visiting angels.

Isaac, born to Abraham by Sarah in his 100th year, was the first of his legitimate descendants.

God demanded that Abraham sacrifice Isaac as a test of faith, but because of Abraham's unquestioning compliance, God permitted him to spare Isaac and rewarded Abraham with a formal renewal of his promise. After Sarah died, Abraham married Keturah. He died at the biblical age of 175.

Abraham's sacrifice of his son Issac stopped by an angel of God

Christians, Muslims, and Jews accept Abraham as an epitome of the man of unswerving faith, a view reflected in the New Testament.

When God informed Abraham that he intended to destroy Sodom and Gomorrah because of the wickedness of their inhabitants, Abraham pleaded with him to spare the cities. Eventually it was agreed that God would spare the cities if he could find only ten righteous men. The ten men could not be found, and God destroyed both cities

According to the Book of Genesis, Abraham was 100 years old when Isaac was born, and Sarah was past 90. Isaac Ben Abraham was born in 1922 BC in Aram, Paktia, Afghanistan. He married Rebekah Bint Bethuel in 1856 BC . They had 11 children.

Abraham's well at Beersheba

According to Genesis, Abraham brought Isaac to Mount Moriah, where, at God's command, Abraham built a sacrificial altar upon which he was commanded to sacrifice his beloved son Isaac. This event was to serve as a test of Abraham's faith.

Abraham tied Isaac and put him on the altar, held the knife over Isaac and was ready to sacrifice his son when, at the last moment, Abraham was stopped by an angel of the Lord. Rather, he was directed to sacrifice instead a nearby ram that was stuck in thickets.

At the age of 75, Isaac moved to *Beer-lahai-roi* after his father died. When the land experienced famine, he removed to the Philistine land of Gerar where his father once lived. This land was still under the control of King Abimelech as it was in the days of Abraham.

He had gone back to all of the wells that his father dug and saw that they were all stopped up with earth. The Philistines did this after Abraham died. So, Isaac unearthed them and began to dig for more wells all the way to Beersheba. He died in Israel when he was 180 years old

Jacob Ibn Isaac - *son of Isaac Ben Abraham* - **Afghanistan**

Jacob Ibn Isaac married Zilpah Jacob I in 1789 BC in Afghanistan. He then married Leah Bint Laban and they had 24 children together. He then had one son with Rachel Bint Laban. He had 10 brothers.

Jacob has a dream during his flight from his brother Esau. The bible recounts *"Jacob's dream: "He came upon a certain place and stopped there for the night, for the sun had set. Taking one of the stones of that place, he put it under his head and lay down in that place. He had a dream; a stairway was set on the ground and its top reached to the sky, and angels of God were going up and down on it. And the Lord was standing beside him...* Jacob awoke from his sleep and said, ... *"How awesome is this place! This is none other than the abode of God and that is the gateway to heaven"* (Genesis 28:10-18).

The location of this event is believed to be Mount Moriah. The site which some would later claim was the "navel of the world". At the summit of Mount Moriah is the "Foundation Stone," the symbolic fundament of the world's creation, and reputedly the site of the Temple's Holy of Holies, the supreme embodiment of the relationship between God and the people of Israel.

Mount Moriah is the name of the elongated north-south stretch of land lying between Kidron Valley and "Hagai" Valley, between Mount Zion to the west and the Mount of Olives to the east.

Near Luz en route to Haran, Jacob experienced a vision of a ladder, or staircase, reaching into heaven with angels going up and down it, commonly referred to as **"Jacob's ladder"**. He

heard the voice of God, who repeated many of the blessings upon him, coming from the top of the ladder.

According to Rashi, the ladder signified the exiles that the Jewish people would suffer before the coming of the Jewish Messiah: the angels that represented the exiles of Babylonia, Persia, and Greece each climbed up a certain number of steps, paralleling the years of the exile, before they "fell down"; but the angel representing the last exile, that of Rome or Edom, kept climbing higher and higher into the clouds. Jacob feared that his descendants would never be free of Esau's domination, but God assured him that at the End of Days, Edom too would come falling down.

In the morning, Jacob awakened and continued on his way to Haran, after naming the place where he had spent the night "Bethel", "God's house".

Judah Ben Israel - *son of* Jacob *ben Isaac* – Israel

Judah Ben Israel married Tamar in 1739 BC. They had 10 children during their marriage. Judah is the fourth son of the patriarch Jacob and his first wife, Leah. His full brothers are Reuben, Simeon and Levi (all older), and Issachar and Zebulun (younger) and one full sister Dinah, he has six half-brothers.

Judah's brother Joseph receives a "Coat of Many Colors" from his father Jacob

Following his birth, Judah's next appearance is in *Gen 37*, when he and his brothers cast Joseph into a pit out of jealousy after Joseph approaches them, flaunting a coat of many colors, while they are working in the field. It is Judah who spots a caravan of Ishmaelites coming towards them, on its way to Egypt and suggests that Joseph be sold to the Ishmaelites rather than killed. (*Gen.* 37:26-28, "What profit is it if we slay our brother and conceal his blood? ... Let not our hand be upon him, for he is our brother, our flesh.")

Judah marries the daughter of Shua, a Canaanite. Genesis chapter 38 Judah and his wife have three children, Er, Onan, and Shelah. Er marries Tamar, but God kills him because he "was wicked in the sight of the Lord" (*Gen.* 38:7). Tamar becomes Onan's wife in accordance with custom, but he too is killed after he refuses to father children for his older brother's childless widow, and spills his seed instead. Although Tamar should have married Shelah, the remaining brother, Judah did not consent, and in response Tamar deceives Judah into having intercourse with her by pretending to be a prostitute. When Judah discovers that Tamar is pregnant he prepares to have her killed, but recants and confesses when he finds out that he is the father (*Gen.* 38:24-26).

Meanwhile, Joseph rises to a position of power in Egypt. Twenty years after being betrayed, he meets his brothers again without them recognizing him. The youngest brother, Benjamin, had remained in Canaan with Jacob, so Joseph takes Simeon hostage and insists that the brothers return with Benjamin. Judah offers himself to Jacob as surety for Benjamin's safety, and manages to persuade Jacob to let them take Benjamin to Egypt. When the brothers return, Joseph tests them by demanding the enslavement of Benjamin. Judah pleads for Benjamin's life, and Joseph reveals his true identity.

Judah is the 9th Great Grandson of Solomon, King of Israel

King Solomon exhibits his wisdom

Zarah ben Judah – son of Judsah ben Israel – **Israel**

Zarah be Judah married Electra One Pleides in Eygpt. They had 21 children. He had nine brothers.

The story of Zara's conception takes the entire thirty-eighth chapter of Genesis. His mother Tamar was the wife of Judah's

oldest son Er. Er died without giving her any children. Judah required his next oldest son [Onan] would keep Er's line alive by her. Onan, however, spilled his semen on the ground; he did this repeatedly to prevent her from conceiving.

As a result of this sin in God's eyes, God kill him, just as he killed his older brother Er. As the custom of the time required, Judah promised that his son Shelah, when he was old enough, would do the family duty by her. But when Shelah was old enough Judah balked

By this time Judah was widowed. So Tamar, with cunning, sat at the gate of a city where Judah traveled, playing the role of a temple prostitute. Having compromised Judah in this fashion, she tricked him into leaving his signet ring as a pledge for her fee. So, when she conceived she was called out as an immoral woman to be stoned. She showed Judah's signet ring and revealed that the man to whom this ring belongs is the father

Tamar had fooled Judah by remaining veiled in the transaction. Judah seeing the justice in the outcome acknowledged that he was that man, he could not deny it, and he declared that she was more righteous than he.

So she bore twin sons by Judah. In delivery, Zara pushed his hand out of the womb first. The midwife tied a red string on it to keep track of the first borne. However his brother Perez broke through ahead of Zara, and was born first.

Perez, the first born, is related to Joseph of Nazareth, husband of Mary, mother of Jesus Christ

Perez became a direct ancestor in the genealogy of Christ [Matthew 1:3] as followed through the line of Joseph. Zara became the father of Darda [Dara 1 Chr. 2:6] for which the Dardanians were named. Darda is said to have founded Dardania on

Jesus Christ's Genealogy
Matthew 1:1-17

Patriarchs	Monarchy	After Deportation
Abraham	Solomon of Uriah	Jeconiah
Isaac	Rehoboam	Shealtiel
Jacob	Abijah	Zerubbabel
Judah	Asa	Abihud
Perez by Tamar	Jehoshaphat	Eliakim
Hezron	Joram	Azor
Ram	Uzziah	Zadok
Amminadab	Jotham	Achim
Nahshon	Ahaz	Eliud
Salmon	Hezekiah	Eleazar
Boaz by Rahab	Manasseh	Matthan
Obed by Ruth	Amon	Jacob
Jesse	Josiah	Joseph the husband of Mary,
David the king	Jeconiah . . . at the time of	by whom Jesus was born, who
	the deportation to Babylon.	is called the Messiah.

Mount Ida [modern Turkey] north of the Isle of Lesbos and south east of Dardanelles. Greek mythology attributes the siring of Dardan to Zeus.

Genesis 38: 30, "And afterward came out his brother, that had the scarlet thread upon his hand: and his name was called Zarah." The Zarah line of the Judah tribe left Egypt hundreds of years before Moses. As those migrating men of the Zarah tribe sailed west in the ships of Dan (the tribe of Dan), they left their name with Dan's name

The island of Zar-Din-ia is today; Sardinia as we call it, west of Italy. The tribe of Zarah settled the Ancient City of Zara-gossa, on the Ebro River in Spain, hence the city name. "Gaza" means "strong" in Hebrew, Zara-goza is "Zerah's stronghold."

The poet Homer's: "Illiad" tells the story of the Israelite quarrel. Prince Paris from Troy, a Zarahite Prince had returned home to Troy with Helen the wife of Menelaus the King of the Danaan city of Sparta, in Greece. That began the 10 years of the Trojan Wars, when the King launched a thousand ships of Dan to attack Troy, to get his wife back.

Remember that Troy was founded by Darda a Zarahite, of Judah...Paris the Trojan, had been in Sparta negotiating a Peace treaty when he came to love Helen...The woman whose face launched a thousand ships. The City of love was named for her. Paris, in France was named for that famous Trojan warrior who loved her so much and began the Trojan Wars.

Helen of Troy

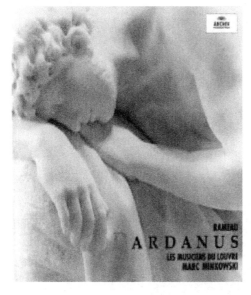

ARDANUS

He was born in 1387 in Egypt. He married Batia Princess of Troy and they had 17 children together. He then had two sons with Batea Teucri. He died at Egypt in 1414 BC

In I Chronicles 2 we read of the line of Judah: "The sons of Judah were Er, Onan, and Shelah. These three were born to him by the daughter of Shua, the Canaanitess...And Tamar, his [Judah's] daughter-in-law, bore him Perez and Zerah. All the sons of Judah were five...The sons of Zerah were Zimri, Ethan Heman, Calcol, and Dara -- five of them in all." (Verses 3-6).

The Bible also spells Dara as "Darda." An examination of some of the historical clues reveals that there lived in Egypt -- during the time of the bondage of the Israelites -- a man named Darda. Some claim "Darda, "the Egyptian," (son of Zarah) to be "Dardanus," the Egyptian Founder of Troy."

Hecataeus of Abdera, a fourth-century B.C. Greek historian, states that "Now the Egyptians say that also after these events [the plagues of Exodus] a great number of colonies were spread from Egypt all over the inhabited world. They say also that those who set forth with Danaus, likewise from Egypt, settled what is practically the oldest city of Greece, Argos, and that the nations of the Colchis in Pontus and that of the Jews (remnant of Judah), which lies between Arabia and Syria, were founded as colonies by certain emigrants from their country [Egypt]; and this is the reason why it is a long-established institution among these peoples to circumcise their male children, the custom having been brought over from Egypt. Even the Athenians, they say, are colonists from Sais in Egypt." (Quoted from *Diodorus of Sicily*. G. H. Oldfather, 1933. Vol. I, bks. I-II, 1-34, p. 91).

While migrations of "circumcised" aliens from Egypt to Greece and Pontus are noted by Hecataeus of Abdera, there is no mention of Dardanus or Darda. This is because Dardanus left Egypt before the Exodus: "Dardanus is said to have built troy about thirty-four years before the exodus." (*British History Traced from Egypt and Palestine*, by L.G.A. Roberts, p. 27).

The Migration of Dardanus
The early migration of Darda is noted in the book *How Israel Came to Britain*: Actually, groups of Israelites began to migrate

Migration of Dardanus

away from the main body before the Israel nation was formed -- while, as a people, they were still in bondage in Egypt. One of these groups under the leadership of Calcol, a prince of the tribe of Judah, went westward across the Mediterranean eventually settling in Ulster [Ireland]. Another, under the leadership of Dardanus, a brother of Calcol, crossed to Asia Minor to found the Kingdom later known as Troy.

Chapter Nine

Out of Biblical Records Into
Greek Mythology

Until this point our ancestral written record was found in the
Hebrew Bible or the Old Testament of the Christian Bible. Now
the record flows into Greek and Roman Mythology.

Erichthonius "The Dardanian" King of Troy *son of Dardanus
Dardania* - **Rameses, Goshen, Egypt**

"The Dardanian"
King of Troy

Erichthonius "The Dardanian"
King of Troy married Astyoche
"Queen of Trojans", of Acadia aka
Astvocho of DARDANIA in
Turkey. They had 11 children.

The mythical King Erichthonius
/ɛrɪkˈθoʊniəs/ of Dardania was the
son of Dardanus, King of
Dardania, and Batea, (although
some legends say his mother was
Olizone, descendant of Phineus).
He is said to have enjoyed a
peaceful and prosperous reign.

153

Fundamentally, all that is known of this Erichthonius comes from Homer, who says .

Dardanos had a son, king Erichthonios, who was wealthiest of all men living; he had three thousand mares that fed by the water meadows, they and their foals with them. Boreas was enamored of them as they were feeding, and covered them in the semblance of a dark-maned stallion. Twelve filly foals did they conceive and bear him, and these, as they sped over the fertile plain, would go

bounding on over the ripe ears of wheat and not break them; or again when they would disport themselves on the broad back of Ocean they could gallop on the crest of a breaker.
Erichthonios begat Tros, king of the Trojans, and Tros had three noble sons, Ilos, Assarakos, and Ganymede who was comeliest of mortal men; wherefore the gods carried him off to be Zeus' cupbearer, for his beauty's sake, that he might dwell among the immortals.

John Tzetzes and one of the scholia to Lycophron call his wife Astyoche, daughter of Simoeis. *The Bibliotheca also adds Erichthonius' older brother Ilus, who died young and childless; presumably a doublet of the other Ilus, grandson of Erichthonius, eponym of Troy.*

Strabo (13.1.48) records, but discounts, the claim by "some more recent writers" that *Teucer came from the deme of Xypeteones in Attica, supposedly called Troes (meaning Trojans) in mythical times.* These writers mentioned that Erichthonius appears as founder both in Attica and the Troad, and may be identifying the two. Erichthonius reigned for forty six or, according to others, sixty five years and was succeeded by his son Tros.

He was King Solomon's 12th Great Grandson

Tros Trois Acadia King of Troy Dardania - *son of Erichthonius* *"The Dardanian" King of Troy* – **Troy**

The ancient city of Troy

Tros Trois Acadia King of Troy Dardania married Callirhoe of Teucri in 1339. They had 19 children during their marriage. Tros succeeded his father Erichthonius to the throne. He gave his name to the land (Troad) and to the people living in the Troad (Trojans).

In Greek mythology, Tros was a ruler of Troy and the son of Erichthonius by Astyoche (daughter of the river god Simoeis) or of Ilus I, from whom he inherited the throne. Tros was the father of three sons: Ilus, Assaracus, and Ganymedes. He is the eponym of Troy, also named *Ilion* for his son Ilus. Tros's wife was said to be Callirrhoe, daughter of the river god Scamander, or Acallaris, daughter of Eumedes.

When Zeus abducted Ganymedes, Tros grieved for his son. Sympathetic, Zeus sent Hermes with two horses so swift they could run over water. Hermes also assured Tros that Ganymede was immortal and would be the cupbearer of the gods, a position of great distinction.

In variant versions Ganymede is son of Laomedon son of Ilus son of Tros; yet others call him son of Ilus, Erichthonius or Assaracus. It was from Tros that the Dardanians were called Trojans and the land named the Troad.

Ilus King of Troy - *son of Tros Trois Acadia King of Troy Dardania,* **Troy**

Ruins of the walls of Troy

Ilus King of Troy married Eurydice of Troy in 1286 in Turkey. They had 20 children during their marriage. He had 14 brothers and four sisters.

In Greek Mythology Ilus is the founder of the city called *Ilios* or *Ilion* to which he gave his name. When the latter became the chief city of the Trojan people it was also often called *Troy*, the name by which it is best known today.

Ilus was son and heir to Tros of Dardania and brother of Assaracus and Ganymede. He won the wrestling prize at games held by the King of Phrygia and received fifty youths and maidens as his reward. The king also, on the advice of an oracle, gave him a cow and asked him to found a city where it should lie down. Ilus did so.

Ilus then prayed to Zeus for a sign and at once saw the Palladium fallen from heaven and lying before his tent but was immediately blinded for the impiety of looking on the image. He regained his sight after making offerings to Athena.

Ilus preferred his new city of Ilium to Dardania and on his father's death he remained there, bestowing the rule of Dardania on his brother Assaracus instead and so the Trojans were split into two kingdoms.

Laomedon King of Troy - *son of Ilus King of Troy* - **Troy**

Heracles about to kill Laomedon

Laomedon Troy married Strymo Placia bint Scamander Troy and they had 20 children together. He then had one son with Placia Troy Strymo. He had 11 brothers and eight sisters.

Laomedon was a king of Troy in Greek mythology, son of Ilus and grandson of Tros. He was the father of a number of children, including Podarces, who was later better known as Priam, and Hesione. His uncle was Ganymede, who was kidnapped by Zeus and became the cupbearer of the gods on Mount Olympus; to compensate for the kidnapping, Zeus had gifted numerous horses to Laomedon's grandfather, Tros.

After offending Zeus, the gods Apollo and Poseidon were told to serve Laomedon by building the walls of Troy. Laomedon told the gods he would reward them generously, a promise he did not keep in the end. The gods, angry, sent a plague and a sea monster to destroy the city.

After being advised by an oracle, Laomedon planned on sacrificing his daughter Hesione to the sea monster. Heracles, on his way back from the land of the Amazons, told him he would save her, if he were given the horses Zeus had previously offered after the kidnapping of Ganymede. Laomedon agreed and Heracles killed the monster. The king did not keep his promise again, and Heracles punished him by killing all of his sons, except Podarces, who was taken with Hesione to Greece.

Tithonus Troy - *son of Laomedon King of Troy* – **Troy**

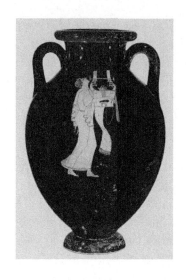

Tithonus Troy married Eos (Aurora) Titan of the dawn in 1235 in Turkey. They had 15 children during their marriage. He had 16 brothers and three sisters.

Eos was known in Roman mythology as Aurora. Tithonus was a Trojan by birth, the son of King Laomedon of Troy by a water nymph named Strymo.

The mythology reflected by the fifth-century vase-painters of Athens envisaged Tithonus as a *rhapsode*, as the lyre in his hand, on an oinochoe (wine jug) of the Achilles Painter. Competitive singing, as in the *Contest of Homer and Hesiod*, is also depicted vividly in the *Homeric Hymn to Apollo* and mentioned in the two *Hymns to Aphrodite*.

Munon Memnon King of Troy - *son of Tithonus Troy* - **Troy**

Memmon gazing at the rising sun

Munon Memnon King of Troy married Troana - Troan Priamsdotter, of Troy in Turkey. They had 10 children during their marriage.

According to ancient Greek poets, Memnon's father Tithonus was snatched away from Troy by the goddess of dawn Eos and was taken to the ends of the earth on the coast of Oceanus. This means he was carried by the east wind and

158

was driven to the western ends of the earth beyond the Ocean or pillars of Hercules. According to Hesiod Eos bore to Tithonus bronzed armed Memnon, the King of the Ethiopians and lordly Emathion.

Zephyrus, god of the west wind, like Memnon was also the 1st born son of Eos (east wind) by another father, Astraeus. According to Quintus Smyrnaeus, Memnon said that the Hesperides on the coast of Oceanus raised him. Memnon dwelling on the western Ocean and his father being driven there would make him the son of dawn (the east) as in the son of Troy rather than the son of eastern Asia as earlier scholars have proposed based on their opinion.

Greek gods of war and destruction

Hesiod makes it clear that the son of Dawn (east) originally means west, making Memnon a colonist (son) from the east and king of the west. And this actually makes the most sense, because as Eos the Dawn Goddess rises from the east before her father Hyperion (the sun) she journeys to the western ends of the earth were she and her father the Sun God sleeps.

To the knowledge of the Greeks the farthest west ended at the land of Atlas towards the Hesperides on the African coast south of the Atlantic Ocean. There is a statue of Memnon west of Luxor in Egypt known today as the Colossi of Memnon. According to the ancient Greek historians this statue of Memnon made a sound at morning time that meant Memnon was speaking to his mother Dawn as she rises in the east while he dwells in the west, making him the son of dawn (east) and ruler of the west.

Thor (Tror) Munonsson, King of THRACE - *son of Munon Memnon King of Troy* - **Troy**

Thor (Tror) Munonsson, King of THRACE was born in 1200. He married SIBIL Sif bint Memnon of Thrace and they had one son together. He then had two sons from another relationship. He had seven brothers and two sisters.

Where was Thrace? Ancient Greek mythology has Thrace geographically centered on the modern borders of Bulgaria, Greece, and Turkey.

Thor King of Trojans Thrace was born in around - 1189 at Troy, Turkey. Thor is a prominently mentioned god throughout the recorded history of the Germanic peoples, from the Roman occupation of regions of Germania, to the tribal expansions of the Migration Period.

During the Viking Age, when, in the face of the process of the Christianization of Scandinavia, the emblems of Thor's hammer, "Mjölnir", were worn in defiance. Norse pagan personal names containing the name of Thor bear witness to his popularity.

Into the modern period, Thor continued to be acknowledged in rural folklore throughout Germanic regions. Thor is frequently referred to in place names including the day of the week Thursday, "Thor's day.

Story of Thor and his Goats

In chapter 21 of the *Prose Edda* book *Gylfaginning*, the enthroned figure of High divulges that the god Thor has two goats that drive his chariot and that these goats bear the names Tanngnjóstr and Tanngrisnir.

In chapter 44, the enthroned figure of Third reluctantly relates a tale in which Thor and Loki are riding in Thor's chariot, pulled by his two goats. Loki and Thor stop at the home of a peasant farmer, and there they are given lodging for a night. Thor slaughters his goats, skins them and puts them in a pot. When the goats are cooked, Loki and Thor sit down for their evening meal.

Thor invites the peasant family to share the meal with him and they do so. At the end of the meal, Thor places the skins of the goat on the opposing side of the fire and tells the peasants to throw the bones of the goats on to the goatskins. The peasant's son Þjálfi takes one of the goat ham-bones and uses a knife to split it open, breaking the bone to get to the marrow.

After staying the night, Thor wakes up and gets dressed before the break of dawn. Thor takes his hammer Mjöllnir, raises it, and blesses the goat skins. Resurrected, the goats stand, but one of the two goats is lame in the hind leg. Noting this new lameness, Thor exclaims that someone has mistreated the bones of his goats; that someone broke the ham-bone during the meal the night before.

Everyone can imagine how terrified the peasant must have been when he saw Thor making his brows sink down over his eyes; as for what could be seen of the eyes themselves, he thought he would collapse at just the very sight. Thor clenched his hands on the shaft of the hammer so that the knuckles went white, and the peasant did as one might expect, and his entire household, they cried out fervently, begged for grace, offered to atone with all their possessions.

At realizing how terrified he has made the peasants, Thor calms down and from them accepted a settlement of their children Þjálfi and Röskva. The two children become his servants and have remained so since. Leaving the goats behind, the four then set out for the land of Jötunheimr.[9] The goats are again mentioned in chapter 48, where Thor is described as setting out to Midgard, the realm of mankind, in the form of a young boy, without goats or companions.

In chapter 75 of the *Prose Edda* book *Skáldskaparmál*, the names of both goats appear among a list of names for goats.

An Ancient Fishing Tale – *A Real Whopper!*

One of four Ancient carving depicting Thor's fishing trip

Thor went out of Asgard disguised as a youth and came in the evening to a giant called Hymir. Thor stayed there that night. At daybreak Hymir got up and dressed and prepared to go deep sea fishing in a rowboat. Thor sprang up and asked Hymir to let him go rowing with him. Hymir said that he would not be much help, as he was such a scrap of a young fellow: "You'll catch cold if I sit as long and as far out to sea as I usually do."

Thor, however, said he would be able to row a long way out from the shore, and that it wasn't certain that he would be the first to demand to be rowed back. He became so angry with the giant that he was ready to set the hammer ringing on his head. He controlled himself, however, as he intended to try his strength in another place. He asked Hymir what they were to take as bait, but

Hymir told him to get his own. Then Thor turned away to where he saw a herd of oxen belonging to Hymir. He selected the biggest ox, one called Sky-Bellower, and struck off its head.

Thor took the ox-head on board, sat down in the stern, and rowed. Hymir thought they made rapid progress from his rowing. Hymir sat in the bow, and together they rowed until they came to the place where Hymir was accustomed to sit and catch flat fish. Thor said he wanted row much farther out, and they had another bout of fast rowing. Then Hymir said that they had come so far out that it would be dangerous to sit there on account of the Midgard Serpent.

Thor's war hammer

Thor, however, declared his intention of rowing for a bit yet, and did so, and Hymir was not at all pleased at that. When Thor shipped his oars, he made ready a very strong line and a large hook. He baited the hook with the ox-head and flung it overboard. The Midgard Serpent snapped at the ox-head, and the hook stuck fast in the roof of its mouth. It jerked away so hard that both Thor's fists knocked against the gunwale. Then

Thor grew angry and, exerting all his divine strength, dug in his heels so hard that both legs went through the boat until he was digging his heels in on the sea bottom. He drew the serpent up on board, staring straight at it. The serpent glared back, belching poison. The giant Hymir turned pale with fear when he saw the serpent and the sea trembling in and out of the vessel too. At the very moment that Thor gripped his hammer and raised it aloft, the giant fumbled for his bait knife and cut Thor's line off at the gunwale. The serpent sank back into the sea. Thor flung his hammer after it and people say that this struck its head off in the waves; but the truth is that the Midgard Serpent is still alive and is lying in the ocean.

Thor clenched his fist and gave Hymir a box on the ear so that he fell overboard head first, but Thor himself waded ashore.

Loridi (Vingeher,Hiloritha) Hloritha Trorsson King of Troy - *son of Thor Munonsson, King of THRACE* - **Troy**

Loidi Hloritha King of Trojans was born to Vingener King of Trojans in Troy about 350BC. Hloritha had one brother: Moda

(Modi) King of Trojans and one son: Einrida King of Trojans.

Lóriði is the forefather of Norse rulers, according to the prologue of the *Prose Edda*. King Loridi does not appear in any other instance of Norse mythology.

The author of the *Prose Edda*, Snorri Sturluson, was a Christian and he used the prologue to explain how the Norse pagans came to believe what they did. He theorizes that many of the heroes from ancient city of Troy came to Scandinavia and were revered as gods and demigods.

The Gods in Norse Mythology and the Kings of Troy
From the *Prose Edda*, tales from Norse mythology.
Near the earth's centre was made that goodliest of homes and haunts that ever have been, called Troy, even that which we call Turkland. This abode was much more gloriously made than others, and fashioned with more skill of craftsmanship in manifold wise, both in luxury and in the wealth, which was there in abundance.

There were twelve kingdoms and one High King, and many sovereignties belonged to each kingdom; in the stronghold were twelve chieftains. These chieftains were in every manly part greatly above other men that have ever been in the world.

One king among them was called Múnón or Mennón; and he was wedded to the daughter of the High King Priam, her who was called Tróán; they had a child named Trór, whom we call Thor.

He was fostered in Thrace by a certain war-duke called Lóríkus; but when he was ten winters old he took unto him the weapons of his father. He was as goodly to look upon, when he came among other men, as the ivory that is inlaid in oak; his hair was fairer than gold. When he was twelve winters old he had his full measure of strength; then he lifted clear of the earth ten bear-skins all at one time; and then he slew Duke Lóríkus, his foster-father, and with him his wife Lórá, or Glórá, and took into his

own hands the realm of Thrace, which we call Thrúdheim.

Then he went forth far and wide over the lands, and sought out every quarter of the earth, overcoming alone all berserks and giants, and one dragon, greatest of all dragons, and many beasts. In the northern half of his kingdom he found the prophetess that is called Síbil, whom we call Sif, and wedded her. The lineage of Sif I cannot tell; she was fairest of all women, and her hair was like gold.

Their son was Lóridi, who resembled his father; his son was Einridi, his son Vingethor, his son Vingener, his son Móda, his son Magi, his son Seskef, his son Bedvig, his son Athra (whom we call Annarr), his son Ítermann, his son Heremód, his son Skjaldun (whom we call Skjöld), his son Bjáf (whom we call Bjárr), his son Ját, his son Gudólfr, his son Finn, his son Fríallaf (whom we call Fridleifr); his son was he who is named Vóden, whom we call Odin: he was a man far-famed for wisdom and every accomplishment. His wife was Frígídá, whom we call Frigg.

Einridi (Einrida Eindrida Eredei) LORIDESSON - *son of Loridi (Vingeher,Hiloritha) Hloritha Trorsson King of Troy* - **Troy**

Einrida King of Trojans was born in Troy about 320 BC. He had one son, Vingeher King of Troy and one brother

Vingethor (Vingethior) Vingithor EINRIDISSON - *son of Einridi (Einrida Eindrida Eredei) LORIDESSON* - **Minor, Yakutia, Russia**

Vingethor (Vingethior) Vingithor EINRIDISSON was born in 370 in Minor, Yakutia, Russia, the child of Einridi (Einrida Eindrida Eredei. He died in Minor, Yakutia, Russia. He had four children with Baltsa Vingethor and three children with Vingethor.

166

The Trojan Horse

The tale Trojan Horse is from the Trojan War and is about the subterfuge the Greeks used to enter the city of Troy to win the war. In the canonical version, after a fruitless 10-year siege, the Greeks constructed a huge wooden horse, and hid a select force of men inside. The Greeks pretended to sail away, and the Trojans pulled the horse into their city as a victory trophy.

That night the Greek force crept out of the horse and opened the gates for the rest of the Greek army, which had sailed back under cover of night. The Greeks entered and destroyed the city of Troy, decisively ending the war.

The Trojan Horse in the city of Troy

Vingener Vinginer II VINGETHORSSON Trojan King - son *of Vingethor Vingethior) Vingithor EINRIDISSON* - **Troy,**

Vingener Vinginer VINGETHORSSON Trojan King was born in 340 in Canakkale, Turkey. He married Astyoche De Acadia II in Turkey. They had four children during their marriage. He died in Canakkale, Turkey He had one son, Moda of Troy

Moda (Mode) VINGENERSSON Trojan King *son of Vingener*
Vinginer II
VINGETHORSSON
Trojan King – **Troy**

Moda (Mode)
VINGENERSSON
Trojan King married
Lady Sceldwa DeTroy in
Greece. They had six
children during their
marriage. He had two
brothers and one sister.

Mogi (Magi, Mage)
Magi Modasson King
of Troy - *son of Moda*
(Mode)
VINGENERSSON
Trojan King - **Troy**

Mogi (Magi, Mage)
Magi Modasson King
of Troy was born in
600 in Canakkale,
Turkey. He had four
sons and one daughter
with Einridi of Troy.
He died in Canakkale,
Turkey. He had five
brothers.

169

Chapter Ten

Trojan Origins of European Royalty!

The **present-day royal lines of Northwestern Europe and Great Britain are all related to DAN I OF DENMARK**. Who was Dan, otherwise known as ODIN?

Tradition and history records the existence of Three Famous Men who bore the name "ODIN." The first, according to author J. Garner, was known as Wodan and "is the same as the Odin of the Scandinavians." He writes:

It would also appear that Wodan, or Odin, who seems to be identified with those gods Whom Cuish was the human original, had a son "Balder," who was slain by Loki, the spirit of evil, just as Osiris was slain by Ttphon, the spirit of evil. Just also as the deaths of Osiris, Bacchus, Thammuz, etc., are Lamented, so is Balder lamented by his mother, Freya or Frigga, who was told by Hela, the goddess of Hell, that he would be restored to life if everything on earth wept for him. Again, just as the war god Mars or Mergal was another manifestation of the younger Babalonian god, so "Thor," the war god of the Scandinavians, was another son of Odin...Odin, Freya and Thor, in short, are the Scandanavian trinity, corresponding to the Egyptian Trinity, Osiris, IRIS AND HORUS, and other forms of the same Trinity, and like Horus, Apollo and Chrishna, Thor is

represented as bruising the head of the serpent. -- **The Worship of the Dead**.

The eighth king in descent from PRIAM was DANUS I or ODIN (VOTAN) first king of Denmark and reigned from 1040-999.

DANUS I WAS THEREFORE A TROJAN OF THE LINE OF JUDAH.

S. Gusten Olson recognizes this link in the line of ODIN: "*It is commonly accepted that ALL the ruling families of the North [Northwestern Europe] definitely date BACK TO ODIN. Odin is DESCENDED FROM THE TROJAN LINE OF KINGS.* (**The Incredible Nordic Origins**. Nordica S. F. Ltd., Kent, England. 1981, p. 87).

The December, 1981 issue of **The Link** discusses the royal lines of northern Europe and their LINK to the mysterious ODIN:

The varied collection of sagas, poetry and prose which comprises the early literature of the northern nations of Europe contains much interesting and valuable historical material, although it is often difficult to separate the fanciful from the factual. The REPEATED assertions and implications that the FAMILIES DESCENDED FROM ODIN (or WODEN) derive from THE ANCIENT TROJAN KINGS (often thought to belong to the fanciful category) may indeed prove to have FIRM FOUNDATION IN TRUTH.

Several factors provide evidence which is HARMONIOUS with such a claim.

Ancient classical and extra-biblical sources indicate that the TROJAN KINGS were of the ROYAL LINE OF JUDAH and that they were closely related to other ROYAL FAMILIES IN IONIA, GREECE AND CRETE. The early British king-line is traditionally DESCENDED THROUGH THE TROJAN KINGS, and the kings of Ireland are stated to have sprung from the MILESIAN ROYAL FAMILY IN IONIA into which "Pharaoh's daughter" married.

Accepting these sources, the royal families of the northern nations of Europe -- Irish-Scottish, Early British, Frankish, Norwegian -- are all of the SCEPTRE TRIBE OF JUDAH and the many intermarriages of these royal lines would thus all be within the ONE GREAT ROYAL FAMILY of which so much is prophesied in Scripture. Queen Elizabeth II has stated that she is WODEN-BORN. -- Christian Israel Foundation, Walsall, England, p. 117.

The written history of Denmark properly begins with the FIRST KING to reign over the people in the Danish peninsula -- this was DANUS I! He is also known as DAN I in Danish history and was the SECOND ODIN or VOTAN.

How this ODIN arrived in the Northwest of Europe is noted by Herman L. Hoeh: "*Denmark originally received its name from the TRIBE OF DANAAN. It passed to the king who took the name of the subjects over whom he ruled. KING DAN I commenced his reign IN 1040 [B.C.]. This was the year of the breakup of the German realm. The division of German territory between the three sons of Wolfheim -- Kells, Gall and Hiller -- left the seafarers of the far northwest of Europe without leadership. To fill the void the German and HEBREW inhabitants of DENMARK called upon a SCION OF THE TROJAN HOUSE to reign over them. That scion was DAN I. He lived at that time IN THRACE.*" (**Compendium of World History**, *Vol. II, pp. 43-44*).

Odin answered the call and led a large migration OUT OF THRACE into DENMARK and the neighboring regions. After organizing his new realm and setting up the institutions necessary to underpin a stable government, Odin set out on a trip ACROSS THE SEAS to establish a NEW COLONY.!

DANUS I Seskef Sceaf King of Troy, 1st King of Denmark/Hammond *son of Mogi (Magi,mage) Magi Modasson King of Troy* – **Troy**

DANUS I Seskef Sceaf King of Troy, 1st King of Denmark/Hammond was born in 220 in Canakkale, Turkey.

He is primarily known as Danus I (DAN I) and also ODIN, the first King of Denmark (- 1040 -999). To the Anglo-Saxons he was WODEN, and to the Germans WODAN (WUOTAN) (Votan). He married Sedegetelebab Ollo. They had four children during their marriage. He died in Canakkale, Turkey.

Much has been written of this King:

Writes Herman L. Hoeh: *"He was the FIRST ODIN or VOTAN -- from the Hebrew ADONAI meaning 'lord.' Denmark originally received its name from the TRIBE OF DANAAN. It passed to the king who took the name of the subjects whom he ruled"* Sceaf is mentioned in chronicles tracing the lineage of the English kings.

William of Malmesbury in his *Gesta regum anglorum* wrote: *Sceaf; who, as some affirm, was driven on a certain island in Germany, called Scandza, (of which Jornandes, the historian of the Goths, speaks), a little boy in a skiff, without any attendant, asleep, with a handful of corn at his head, whence he was called Sceaf; and, on account of his singular appearance, being well received by the men of that country, and carefully educated, in his riper age he reigned in a town which was called Slaswic, but at present Haithebi; which country, called old Anglia, whence the Angles came into Britain, is situated between the Saxons and the Goths.*

J. R. R. Tolkien wrote of Sceaf in a poem "King Sheave," which was published after he died. In Tolkien's poem, a ship drifts to the land of the Longobards in the north. It beaches itself and the folk of that country enter and found a young and handsome boy with dark hair asleep with a "sheaf of corn" as his pillow and a harp beside him.

The boy awoke the following day and sang a song in an unknown tongue which drove away all terror from the hearts of those who heard. They made the boy their king, crowning him with a garland of golden wheat. Tolkien's Sheave fathers seven sons from whence came the Danes, Goths, Swedes, Northmen, Franks, Frisians, Swordmen (Brongdingas), Saxons, Swabes, English, and the Langobards.

Far Reaching Realm
King Danus' realm extended far beyond the reaches of the Danish peninsula. The people over whom he ruled were a collection of

tribes, which constituted the greatest sea power of the time -- the Pelasgians or sea people. From the list of sea powers, commented on in Volume I of the Compendium, it is proved that the Pelasgians were Hebrews and their allies. Their chief center of habitation was Palestine.

Denmark was one of several overseas settlements. Israel gained power in 1057, shortly before the break-up of Germany in Europe. They retained it until 972, when Solomon's kingdom in Palestine was split. For the Israelites to have obtained dominion of the sea in 1057 in the Mediterranean and Atlantic presupposes that they already were living along the western shores of Europe before that date.

Danus Settles England
And the Welsh Triad records that in his later years he also settled Israel peaceably in the British Isle (Ynys Pridain -- the Welsh name of the Isle of Britain.) From there, for trading purposes, they

175

spread to the coasts of the continent, which were subject to the the descendants of the German king Cimbrus . That is how Israel in Denmark came to be known by the tribal name of Cymry.

As time elapsed the peninsula of Denmark became a chief area of trade and commerce. It is strategically located to dominate both North and Baltic sea trade. So together with the original German tribes of the Cymry and Dauciones were migrants from Britain. In 1040 the Hebrew Cymry called for a descendant of Judah, a royal scion of the House of Troy, to rule over them.

Danus Settles Denmark

Odin answered the call and led a migration out of Thrace into

Denmark and neighboring regions.(Herman Hoeh. Compendium of World History. Vol. II. Ambassador College, 1963. P. 50).

It was from Thrace that ODIN led THE AGATHYRSI and OTHER TRIBES to northwestern Europe when he founded the Danish kingdom. {S4}. Danus I, or Odin first king of Denmark. Reigned 42 years, 1040-999 B.C.

Danus Settles Scotland

The first permanent settlement of Scotland, for which we have recorded history, begins with the coming of Danus I of Denmark in 1040. When the Cimbric tribes called upon an heir of the Trojan throne to establish his domain in Denmark, Odin responded immediately.

Out of southeastern Europe he marched into Denmark. Coming with him was a mixed tribe known as the Agathyrsi. Agathirsi was their name, declares an old Scottish Chronicle. ("Controversial Issues in Scottish History", by W. H. Gregg, p. 125.) Odin settled them in Scotland under their leader Cruithne -- after whom they were called Cruithnians or Cruithne. Herodotus, the Greek historian, traces the Agathyrsi to their origin in the Scythian plains of what is now the southern Ukraine The

176

Agathyrsi were a mixed race. Various struggles led to a catastrophe among the Agathyrsi who came with Odin. They found themselves without women!

They Reach Ireland Without Women

As a consequence they sought wives among neighboring tribes. They landed in Ireland at the time of the establishment of the Milesian monarchy under Ghede the Herimon (1016-1002). Following a few skirmishess an agreement was reached. The Milesians of Ireland agreed to give wives to the Agathyrsi from their daughters on one condition: that the Agathyrsi would pass on their inheritance through their daughters, not their sons. This was to acknowledge that any royalty which might follow derived kingship from their Milesian wives, not from the Agathyrsi men. On this condition the Agathyrsi departed again for Scotland.

Bedweg Bedwig of Sceaf King of Troy Hammond - *son of DANUS I Seskef Sceaf King of Troy, 1st King of Denmark/Hammond* - **Troy**

King Bedwig Scoffing was able to hold on to all of his father's territory. Learning something from the previous dynasty's failure due to inbreeding, Bedwig instituted a policy of marrying his surplus sons and daughters to whatever tribe was the strongest threat to the Angli. His nine sons married princesses of noble blood among the Saxons, Goths, Geats, Kindaughters to anyone of wealth and power who would pledge to support him. He married his heir, Hwala, to the Jutish chieftain's oldest daughter, the Jutes being restive even in those days. In that way, along with waging wars whenever there was something to be gained, did the House of Sceaf maintain the rank of first among equals in the peninsula and the isles.

177

"These kings maintained their kingdoms in a fit fashion. They were recognized as god-kings, the representatives of the gods on earth. They acted well, and thus were blessed with bountiful harvests. Both gods and men found them just, and the lands of the Anglican Confederation prospered. Although the tribal alliance wasn't called then by that name even though the Angli were the foremost members.

During Hadra's rule a great flood from the ocean came over the land, despoiling the grass and silting the land.

Hwala Gulahwaia King of Troy - *son of Bedweg Bedwig of Sceaf King of Troy Hammond* - **Troy, now Canakkale Province, Marmara, Turkey**

Hwala Gulahwaia King of Troy was born in 95 in Canakkale, Turkey. He had two sons with the Jutish chieftain's oldest daughter. He died in Canakkale,

Hathra Athra Athra Troy - *son of Hwala Gulahwaia King of Troy* - **Marmara**

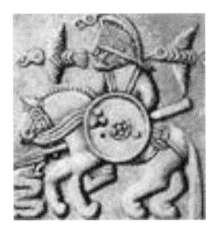

Hathra Athra Athra Troy was born about 145, in Marmara, Balikesir, Turkey. He married Astyoche deDardania in Russia. They had four children during their marriage.

During Hathra's rule, a great flood from the ocean came over the land, despoiling the grass and silting the land. This great flood drove much of the surplus population south to Rome, where they were killed or enslaved. As a result of that flood, the people knew that the gods were displeased, so rule passed to Itermon Hadring.

Itormann Itermon the Trojan King of Troy - *son of Hathra Athra Athra Troy –* **Marmara**

Itormann Flag of Troy

Itormann Itermon the Trojan King of Troy was born in 120 in Marmara, Balikesir, Turkey. He had two sons with Lady Itomann of Troy. He died in Troy.

Heremoed Trojan Troy - *son of Itormann Itermon the Trojan King of Troy* - **Asia,**

Heremoed the Trojan King of Troy was born to Itermon Itormann Itermod Itermann Troy ABT 1930 BC, in Troad, Troy, Greece. Heremoed married Lady King of Troy (born Sceaf). She was born in 75 BC, in Asia, Ghowr, Afghanistan. They had 13 sons, including Bjaed (Bjaf), King of Troy and one daughter.

Bjaed Bjaf, King of Troy - *son of Heremoed Trojan Troy* - **Russia**

Bjaed Bjaf, King of Troy was born in 1950 in Minor, Yakutia, Russia. He has one child with geflon De Danes and two children with Queen Bjaed. He died in Minor, Yakutia, Russia[

Skjold or Scaeldea King of TROY *son of Bjaed Bjaf, King of Troy* - **Troy**

Scaeldea (Sceaf, Skjold) King of Troy was born in Troad, Troy, Greece. He had seven sons with Gefion Dedanes. He died in Marma, Balikesir, Turkey

Sceafa was an ancient Lombardic king in English legend. According to this story, Sceafa appeared mysteriously as a child, coming out of the sea in an empty boat.

The name also appears in the corrupt forms *Seskef*, *Stefius*, *Strephius*, and *Stresaeus*. Though the name has historically been modernized Shava (and Latinized Scefius), J. R. R. Tolkien used the modern spelling *Sheave*.

Many legends exist regardiong Skjold. In the Old English poem *Beowulf* the opening, Scyld is called *Scyld Scefing*, which might mean Scyld descendant of Scef, Scyld son of Scef, or Scyld of the Sheaf.

The *Beowulf* poet does not explain. But after relating in general terms the glories of Scyld's reign, the poet describes Scyld's funeral, how his body was laid in a ship surrounded by treasures, the poet explains:

> They decked his body no less bountifully
> with offerings than those first ones did
> who cast him away when he was a child
> and launched him alone out over the waves.

No other source relates anything similar about Scyld/Skjöld, so it cannot be known whether this is a case of similar stories being told about two different heroes or whether originally separate figures have been confused with one another.

Chapter Ten

Beginning of the Christian Era

Beowa or **Beaw** KING of Troy *son of Skjold or Scaeldea King of TROY* - **Troy**

He was born Ghowr, Afghanistan. He had five sons. He died in 70 in Turkey, at the age of 60. Connections have been proposed between the figure of Beowa and the hero Beowulf of the poem of the same name and English folk song figure John Barleycorn.

Some scholars make a connection between the mythical figure of Beowa and the legendary Beowulf. Because the two characters possess many of the same attributes, it has been suggested that "a god Beowa, whose existence in myth is certain, became confused or blended with Beowulf." Another possibility is that the (first) scribe responsible for the text conflated them: at the beginning of the poem, there is a character called Beowulf (not the Beowulf of the title) who appears in the family tree of Scyld Scefing; this "Beowulf" is frequently changed to "Beow."

Taetwa Tecti King of Troy - *son of Beowa or Bean or Beaw KING OF Troy* – **Troy**

When Tecti Taetwa King of Troy the Trojan was born, his father Beawa was 30. He had two sons with Lady Taetwa Tecti. He died in 100 in Asia, Ghowr, Afghanistan, at the age of 90.

Geata Jat "the Trojan" of Asgard King of Troy *son of Taetwa Tecti Troy* - **Troy**

When Geata Jat "the Trojan" of Asgard King of Troy was born in 60 in Asia, Ghowr, Afghanistan, his father, Taetwa, was 35. He had two sons. He died about 155, at the age of 95 in Scandanavia.

Godwulf Trojan of Asgard - *son of Geata Jat of Asgard King of Troy*

When Godwulf was born in 80 his father, Geata, was 25. He was born in Asia, Ghowr, Afghanistan. He had 10 sons and two daughters. He died in Asia, Ghowr, Afghanistan, having lived 83 years.

Anglo-Saxon royal genealogies refer to the genealogies of the pre-Viking Anglo-Saxon kingdoms of Britain. These trace the royal families through legendary kings and heroes and ancestor of their clan. In most cases leads to the god-hero of the Anglo-Saxon peoples, Woden. Others will continue the pedigrees **back to patriarchs Noah and Adam**.

He is mentioned in *Historia Britonum*;
In the meantime, three vessels, exiled from Germany, arrived in Britain. They were commanded by Horsa and Hengist, brothers, and sons of Wihtgils. Wihtgils was the son of Witta; Witta of Wecta; Wecta of Woden; Woden of Frithowald; Frithowald of Frithuwulf; Frithuwulf of Finn; Finn of Godwulf; Godwulf of Geat, who, as they say, was the son of a god, not of the omnipotent God and our Lord Jesus Christ (who before the beginning of the world, was with the Father and the Holy Spirit, co-eternal and of the same substance, and who, in compassion to human nature, disdained not to assume the form of a servant), but the offspring of one of their idols, and whom, blinded by some demon, they worshipped according to the custom of the heathen.

Flocwald Asgard - *son of Godwulf Trojan of Asgard*

When Flocwald Asgard was born about 100 AD his father, GodWulf the Trojan and his wife Flocwald were 20. They had eight children during their marriage. He died in 179 AD at Ad, Indonesia having lived 79 years

There are records and data that say Flocwald led his people north to escape the on-slaught of the Roman hordes.

Finn Trojan Godwulf Gothia - *son of Flocwald Asgard -*
Afghanistan

Finn Of Godwulf was born in 130AD. He had 19 sons and five daughters. He died in 220AD, at the age of 90.

Godwulf or Guðúlfr is a figure from Germanic mythology. In the two surviving sources mentioning the figure he is associated with divine roots

The Icelandic "Prose Edda," asserts that **Godwulf is a descendant of Thor, Sif and Odin.**

Frithuwulf Fredulf Asgard Asia- *son of Finn Trojan Godwulf Gothia* - **Troy, Greece**

Frithuwulf Fredulf Asgard Asia was born in 190, Godwulf in Troy. His mother Hildebur(g)h was born in Fyn, Denmark.

Frithuwulf married Finn Asgard Asia. They had three children including their son: King Freothalaf Frealaf "Friallaf" King of Trojans of Asgard. He then married Beltsa the Trojan Lady of Asgard and they had one son together. He died in 220 in Ad, Maluku, Indonesia.

Gossip from the past

"Finn begat Frithuwulf, who in turn begat Frealaf. Frealaf begat Frithuwald. Great men all." Eldred abruptly stopped speaking. He got to his feet and began pacing the fire, scanning the crowd.

"That sneaky Frisian rascal, King Folc, has named his sons Finn and Frithuwald. He claims that Woden was a Frisian and his ancestor. Well, maybe Woden was indeed Folc's ancestor. Woden loved fighting, drinking, and womanizing, in that close order. Woden passed more than a few times through Frisia.

So I will grant his claim to Woden as an ancestor. But to say that Woden was Frisian born is the height of untruth. I am tempted to beat the next Frisian I meet and tell him to pass the same message on through to the mangy rascal that he has for a king!"

187

Freothalaf Frealaf "Friallaf" King of Trojans of Asgard - *son of Frithuwulf Fredulf Asgard Asia* - **Ghowr, Afghanistan**

Freothalaf Frealaf "Friallaf " King of the Trojans of Asgard was born in 160 in Ghowr, Afghanistan, the child of Finn the Trojan of Godwulf and Hildeburh. He married Freothalaf the Trojan in 181 in Ghowr, Afghanistan. They had one child during their marriage. He died in having lived a long life of 85 years.

About Troy, the Trojans and the Trojan War

Neoptolemus, son of Achilles, kills King Priam

Many Kings of Troy are in the "Mayflower" line. The ancient city of Troy appeared in Greek and Latin literature. Homer first mentioned the story of Troy in Iliad and Odyssey. Later, it became the most popular subject in Greek drama. Homer's great Trojan War that took place about 1200 BC is featured in the 2004 movie "Troy," starring Brad Pitt.

In Greek mythology, the Trojan War was waged against the city of Troy by the Achaeans (Greeks) after Paris of Troy took Helen from her husband Menelaus king of Sparta. This war took place about the same time that Moses was leading the Jews to the Promise Land.

After the Trojan War, the ancient city of Troy was destroyed and abandoned from about 1100-700 BC but the Greeks then re-established it later on. The ancient city of Troy was originally built about 3,000 BC and was finally destroyed for good in 400 AD. after being destroyed at least nine times before.

In the Bronze age, Troy was a great power because of its strategic location between Europe and Asia. In the 3rd and 2nd centuries BC, Troy was a cultural center. About 700 BC, Greek settlers began to occupy the Troas region and Troy was resettled and named as Ilion.

Alexander the Great ruled the area around the 4th century BC. After Romans captured Troy in 85 BC, it was restored partially by Roman general Sulla and named as New Ilium. For many years, people believed that Troy was a city only in tales and never existed. But then it was discovered in 1870 AD by archeologist H. Schlieman. in Hisarlik near Canakkale province, Turkey.

Frithuwold aka Friothulf Frithowald Bor vonDrottnar Asgard Overlord of *son of Freothalaf Frealaf "Friallaf" King of Trojans of Asgard* - **Ghowr, Afghanistan**

Frithuwald Bor Or Fredalat The Asgard King of Saxony, Turkey and Sweden was born in 190 in Asia, Ghowr, Afghanistan. He married Beltsa Trojan Lady Asgard and they had 16 children together.
He died in Uppsala, Sweden at age 85.

Odin Woden Frithuwaldsson - *son of Frithuwold aka Friothulf Frithowald Bor von Drottnar Asgard Overlord* - **Ghowr, Afghanistan**

Odin, King of Scandanavia

Odin Woden Frithuwaldsson was born in 215. He married Friege or Frigg or Frea deSiluria and they had 26 children together. He then had one son with Fjörgyn. Odin died in 300 in Uppsala, Sweden, having lived 85 years.

The most famous of Norse Gods. Odin migrated from Asgard (near Byzantium) and settled in Uppland, Sweden, near present day Stockholm. He died in Uppsala, Sweden at age 85.

All of the Anglo-Saxon and Scandinavian Kings trace their direct male ancestry to Odin.

From the "Prose Edda" (The *Prose Edda*, also known as the *Younger Edda*, *Snorri's Edda* or, historically, simply as *Edda*, is an Old Norse work of literature written in Iceland in the early 13th century. The work is often assumed to have been written, by the Icelandic scholar and historian Snorri Sturluson around the year 1220.)

Odin had the power of divination, and so had his wife, and from this knowledge he found out that his name would be held high in the north part of the world, and honored beyond that of all kings.

For this reason he was eager to begin his journey from Turkey, and he had with him very many people, young and old, men and women, and he had with him many costly things. But wherever they fared over the lands great fame was spoken of them, and they were said to be more like gods than men.

And they stopped not on their journey before they came north into that land which is now called Saxland; there Odin remained a long time, and subjugated the country far and wide.
There Odin established his three sons as a defense of the land.

A 16th-century depiction of Norse gods by Olaus Magnus: from left to right, Frigg, Thor, and Odin

One is named Veggdegg; he was a strong king and ruled over East Saxland. His son was 46 Vitrgils, and his sons were Ritta, the father of Heingest (Hengist), and Sigar, the father of Svebdegg, whom we call Svipdag. Another son of Odin hight Beldegg, whom we call Balder; he possessed the land which now hight Vestfal; his son was Brander, and his son Frjodigar, whom we call Froda (Frode).

His son was Freovit, his son Yvigg, his son Gevis, whom we call Gave. The third son of Odin is named Sigge, his son Verer. From all of these many and great races are descended.

Viking Age to post-Viking Age

In the 11th century, chronicler Adam of Bremen recorded in a scholion of his *Gesta Hammaburgensis Ecclesiae Pontificum* that a statue of Thor, who Adam describes as "mightiest", sat enthroned in the Temple at Uppsala (located in Gamla Uppsala, Sweden) flanked by Wodan (Odin) and "Fricco". Regarding Odin, Adam defines him as "frenzy" (*Wodan, id est furor*) and says that he "rules war and gives people strength against the enemy" and that the people of the temple depict him as wearing armor, "as our people depict Mars". According to Adam, the people of Uppsala had appointed priests to each of the gods, who were to offer up sacrifices, and in times of war sacrifices were made to images of Odin.

In the 12th century, centuries after Norway was "officially" Christianized, Odin was still being invoked by the population, as evidenced by a stick bearing a runic message found among the Bryggen inscriptions, Bergen, Norway. On the stick, both Thor and Odin are called upon for help; Thor is asked to "receive" the reader, and Odin to "own" them

---

Baeldaeg Aesir aka Bael Odinsson - *son of Odin Woden Frithuwaldsson* - **Lake Malaren, Sweden**

Baldr (also Balder, Baldur) is a god in Norse mythology, who is given a central role in the mythology. Despite this his precise function is rather disputed. He is often interpreted as the god of love, peace, forgiveness, justice, light or purity, but was not directly attested as a god of such.

He is the second son of Odin and the goddess Frigg. His twin
brother is the blind god, Höðr. According to *Gylfaginning*, a book
of Snorri Sturluson's Prose Edda, Baldr's wife is Nanna and their
son is Forseti.

In *Gylfaginning*, Snorri relates that Baldr had the greatest ship
ever built, named Hringhorni, and that there is no place more
beautiful than his hall, Breidablik.

Thor Kicks Litr onto Baldr's Burning Ship, illustration
by Emil Doepler (ca. 1905).

In Norse mythology, Hringhorni (Old Norse "ship with a circle on
the stem"[11]) is the name of the ship of the god Baldr, described as
the "greatest of all ships". According to *Gylfaginning*, following
the murder of Baldr by Loki, the other gods brought his body
down to the sea and laid him to rest on the ship. They would have
launched it out into the water and kindled a funeral pyre for Baldr
but were unable to move the great vessel without the help of the
giantess Hyrrokkin, who was sent for out of Jötunheim. She then
flung the ship so violently down the rollers at the first push that
flames appeared and the earth trembled, much to the annoyance of
Thor.

Along with Baldr, his wife Nanna was also borne to the funeral pyre after she had died of grief. As Thor was consecrating the fire with his hammer Mjolnir, a dwarf named Litr began cavorting at his feet. Thor then kicked him into the flames and the dwarf was burned up as well. The significance of this seemingly incidental event is speculative but may perhaps find a parallel in religious ritual. Among other artifacts and creatures sacrificed on the pyre of Hringhorni were Odin's gold ring Draupnir and the horse of Baldr with all its trappings.

In the 12th century, Danish accounts by Saxo Grammaticus and other Danish Latin chroniclers recorded a euhemerized account of his story. Compiled in Iceland in the 13th century, but based on much older Old Norse poetry, the Poetic Edda and the Prose Edda contain numerous references to the death of Baldr as both a great tragedy to the Æsir and a harbinger of Ragnarök. He was killed by Höðr.

Gefion Dedanes daughter *of Baeldaeg Aesir aka Bael Odinsson –*
Denmark

Gefion Dedanes was born and died in Denmark. She had seven sons with Scaeldea (Sceaf Skjold) King Of Troy. She also married Skjold Danes in Denmark.

In Norse mythology, Gefjon is a goddess associated with ploughing, the Danish island of Zealand and virginity.

The "Prose Edda" reports that Gefjon plowed away what is now lake Mälaren, Sweden, and with this land formed the island of Zealand, Denmark. In addition, the "Prose Edda" describes that not only is Gefjon a virgin herself, but that all who die a virgin become her attendants.

Beawa bedwa King of Troy, *son of Gefion Dedanes* - **Ghowr, Afghanistan**

Beawa bedwa King of Troy was born Ghowr, Afghanistan. He had five sons. He died in Turkey, at the age of 60.

Tecti Taetwa King of Troy Trojan, *son of Beawa bedwa King of Troy* – **Afganistan**

Ancient Troy

When Tecti Taetwa King of Troy was born his father, Beawa, was 30. He had two sons with Lady Taetwa Tecti. He died in 100 in Ghowr, Afghanistan, at the age of 60.

Geata Jat King of Troy Trojan *son of Tecti Taetwa King of Troy Trojan* - **Afghanistan**

Geata Jat King of Troy Trojan was born in 65. He had nine sons. He died in 155 in Troy at the age of 90.

Trojan Godwulf *son of Geata Jat King of Troy Trojan* - **Ghowr, Afghanistan**

When Trojan Godwulf was born in 80 his father, Geata, was 15. He married and had five children. He died in 163 in Ghowr, Afghanistan, having lived 83 years

Godwulf or Guðúlfr is a figure from Germanic mythology. In the two surviving sources mentioning the figure he is associated with divine genealogies.

Historia Britonum:
In the 9th century Historia Brittonum Godwulf is mentioned as an ancestor of Horsa and Hengest:

In the meantime, three vessels, exiled from Germany, arrived in Britain. They were commanded by Horsa and Hengist, brothers, and sons of Wihtgils. Wihtgils was the son of Witta; Witta of Wecta; Wecta of Woden; Woden of Frithowald; Frithowald of Frithuwulf; Frithuwulf of Finn; Finn of Godwulf; Godwulf of Geat, who, as they say, was the son of a god, There is some question regarding the ancestor of Godwulf, listed as "Geat" in Historia Brittonum.

Flocwald Asgard *son of Trojan Godwulf* - **Ghowr, Afghanistan**

When Flocwald Asgard was born his father, Trojan Godwulf, and his mother, were 20. He married in Ghowr, Afghanistan and had eight children during the marriage.

He died in 179 Ad lived 79 years.

Finn Of Godwulf *son of Flocwald Asgard* - **Ghowr, Afghanistan**

Finn the Trojan of Godwulf Asia Asgard was born in 130. He had 13 sons and five daughters. He died in 220 in Ad, Maluku, Indonesia, at the age of 90.

He was married to Hildeburh, a sister of the Danish lord Hnæf, and was killed in a fight with Hnæf's lieutenant Hengest after Hnæf was himself killed by Frisians.

A passage from *Beowulf* as translated by Seamus Heaney reads:

"Finn, son of Folcwald, should honour the Danes,..."
A possible reference to a lost tradition on Finn appears in Snorri Sturluson's *Skáldskaparmál*. Snorri talks of the animosity between Eadgils and Onela (which also appears in *Beowulf*), and writes that Aðils (Eadgils) was at war with a Norwegian king named Áli (Onela). Áli died in the war, and Aðils took Áli's helmet, *Battle-boar*, and his horse Raven. The Danish berserkers who had helped him win the war demanded three pounds of gold each in pay, and two pieces of armour that nothing could pierce: the helmet battle-boar, and the mailcoat *Finn's heritage*. They also wanted the famous ring Svíagris. Aðils considered the pay outrageous and refused.

Finn is a central subject of *Finn and Hengest*, a study of the Finnesburg Episode by J. R. R. Tolkien, edited by Alan Bliss and published posthumously in book form in 1982.

Freothalaf the Trojan Åsgard *daughter of Finn Of Godwulf -* Ghowr, Afghanistan

Wife Freothalaf the Trojan Åsgard had nine sons and five daughters with her husband Freothalaf King of the Trojans of Asgard. She had seven brothers and two sisters.

Frithuwald Bor the Asgard King of Saxony, Turkey and Sweden *son of Freothalaf the Trojan Åsgard -* Ghowr, Afghanistan

Frithuwald Bor the Asgard King of Saxony, Turkey and Sweden was born in 190 BC in Ghowr, Afghanistan. He married Beltsa Trojan Lady of Asgar d, Asia and Swedes and they had 16 children together. He then had five sons from another relationship. He died at age 91

Chapter Eleven

Out of Asia, into Europe (Germany)

Old Saxony is the original homeland of the Saxons in the northwest corner of modern Germany and roughly corresponds today with the contemporary Lower Saxony, Westphalia and western Saxony-Anhalt. Adam of Bremen, writing in the eleventh century, compared the shape of Old Saxony to a triangle, and estimated from angle to angle the distance was eight days journey.

Old Saxony

In area Old Saxony was the greatest of the German tribal duchies. It included the entire territory between the lower Elbe and Saale rivers almost to the Rhine. Between the mouths of the Elbe and the Weser it bordered the North Sea. The only parts of the territory which lay across the Elbe were the counties of Holstein and Ditmarsch.

The tribal lands were roughly divided into four kindred groups: the Angrians, along the right bank of the Weser; the Westphalians, along the Ems and the Lippe; the Eastphalians, on the left bank of the Weser; and the Nordalbingians, in modern Schleswig-Holstein. But not even with these four tribal groups was the term of tribal division reached.

For the Saxon "nation" was really a loose collection of clans of kindred stock. For example, the Nordalbingians alone were divided into lesser groups- Holsteiners, Sturmarii, Bardi, and the men of Ditmarsch. Old Saxony is the place from which most of the raids and later colonization's of Britain were mounted.

The region was called "Old Saxony" by the later descendants of Anglo-Saxon migrants to Britain. In Germany the Saxon lands were known simply as "Saxony" (Modern German: Sachsen) and only later came to be called Lower Saxony, to differentiate those original Saxon tribal territories from what became the Kingdom of Saxony or Upper Saxony in territories far to the south-east of the original Saxon homeland. The Anglo-Saxon writer Bede claimed in his work Historia ecclesiastica gentis Anglorum (731) that Old Saxony was the area between the Elbe, the Weser and the Eider in the north and north west of modern Germany and was a territory beyond the borders of the Roman Empire. It has been claimed that the Old Saxons were composed of an aristocracy of nobles, a free warrior class of distinction and renown, leading freemen united and controlled by ancient custom of kindred and clan.

Harderich vonSaxony *son of Frithuwald Bor Or Fredalat The Asgard King of Saxony, Turkey and Sweden – **Sachsen** Germany*

Harderich vonSaxony was born in 111 BC at Saxony, Germany to Frithuwald Lord Bor de Anglo Saxons Asgard and Beltsa "the Trojan" Lady of Asgard (Asia) Queen of the Asgard (born Swedish).

He married Dobiogera Vonwenden in Saxony Germany and they had five children together including Anserich von Saxony. He passed away at age 90.

King Anserich von Saxony *son of Harderich vonSaxony -* **Sachsen, Germany**

King Anserich von Saxony was born in Saxony, Germany. He had one son, Wilki I von Saxony on July 20, 0020. He died in Saxony, Germany in 65 BC.

Wilki I von Saxony *son of King Anserich von Saxony -* **Sachsen, Germany**

Wilki I von Saxony was born on July 20, 0020, in Saxony, Germany, the child of King Anserich. He married and had one child during their marriage. Wilki I died in 90 in Saxony, Germany, at the age of 70.

For most of its history, Germany was not a unified state but a loose association of territorial states that together made up the "Holy Roman Empire of the German Nation". It was a long time until the founding of the German Reich in 1871.

Svarticke von Saxony *son of Wilki I von Saxony* - **Sachsen, Germany**

Svarticke von Saxony was born in 45 in Saxony, Germany, the child of Wilki I von and wife of Wilki I von. He had two sons. He died in 76 in Saxony, Germany, at the age of 31.

Svarticke II of Saxony *son of Svarticke von Saxony* - **Sachsen, Germany**

When Svarticke II of Saxony was born in 70 in Saxony, Germany, his father, Svarticke, was 25. He has one child with Svarticke von Saxony and one more child. He died in 98 in Saxony, Germany, at the age of 50.

In prehistoric times, the territory of Saxony was the site of some of the largest of the ancient Central European monumental temples, dating from the 5th century BC. Notable archaeological sites have been discovered in Dresden and the villages of Eythra and Zwenkau near Leipzig.

Prince Sigward Von Saxony *son of Svarticke II of Saxony –*
Germany

Prince Sigward Von Saxony was born in 95 in Saxony, Germany, the child of Svarticke II of. He married Mrs Sigward in Saxony, Germany. They had three children during their marriage. He died in 140 in Saxony, Germany, at the age of 45.

KING Witekind I Von Saxony *son of Prince Sigward Von*

Saxony - **Germany**

KING Witekind Von Saxony was born in 82 in Saxony, Germany. He married Lady Witekind von Saxony about 144. They had six children during their marriage. He died in 160 in Saxony, Germany, having lived 78 years.

King Wilki vonSaxony *son of KING Witekind I Von Saxony –*
Germany

When King Wilki vonSaxony was born in 145 his father, KING Witekind, was 63. He married and they had one daughter together. He then had five sons with Queen Belsa vonSaxony. He also married Freothelaf Freothelaf. King Wilki died in 190 in Saxony, Germany, at the age of 45.

Marbod King of the Danes von Saxony *son of King Wilki vonSaxony –* **Prussia**

When Marbod King of the Danes von Saxony was born in 185 in Saxony, Germany, his father, King, was 40. He married Julanda Von Saxony and they had two children together. He then had three sons with Beltsea Beltsa Asgard. He died in 256 in Saxony, Germany, at the age of 71.

Bodo (Wodin) King of the Danes von Saxony *son of Marbod King of the Danes von Saxony -* **Sachsen, Germany**

When Bodo (Wodin) King of the Danes von Saxony was born about 229, in Saxony, Germany, his father, Marbod, was 44. He married Queen Frig Von Saxony and they had 14 children together. He then had one son with his wife. He died in 300 in Saxony, Germany, at the age of 71.

Witt VON SAXONY *son of Bodo (Wodin) King of the Danes von Saxony -* **Sachsen, Germany**

When Witt VON SAXONY was born about 314, in Saxony, Germany. He had one son with his first wife. He then had one son with Bodo Von Saxony. He then married Geva Eisteinsdatter and they had four children together. Witt died about 400, in Saxony, Germany, having lived 86 years.

Witigislus Saxony *son of Witt VON SAXONY* - **Sachsen, Germany**

King Witigislus Saxony was born in 352 in Saxony, Germany. He has three children with his wife and one more child in another relationship. He died in 434 in Kent, having lived 82 years.

Hengest "The Jute" King of Kent *son of Witigislus Saxony* - **Sachsen, Germany**

Tunbridge Castle

Hengest "The Jute" King of Kent was born about 392, in Saxony, Germany. He had one daughter. He later married Elsa 'Queen of Kent' Horsa and they had three children together.

He is the subject of Anglo-Saxon, and subsequently British, legend, which records he and his brother Horsa who led the Angle, Saxon, and Jutish armies that conquered the first territories of Great Britain in the 5th century AD. Hengist, through his son is traditionally listed as the founder of the Kingdom of Kent.

He died in 474 in Tonbridge Castle, Kent, England having lived 82 years.

Hartwaker King of Saxony *son of Hengest "The Jute" King of Kent* - **Sachsen, Germany**

When *Hartwaker King of Saxony was born in 418 in Saxony, Germany, his father, Hengest, was 26. He married Horstus Horsta von Saxony and they had eight children together. He also married Elsa in Saxony, Germany. He died in 480 in Saxony, Germany, at the age of 62.

HUTUGAST HATTWIGATE King of Saxony *son of Hartwaker King of Saxony* - **Sachsen, Germany**

When HUTUGAST HATTWIGATE King of Saxony was born in 460 in Saxony, Germany, his father was 42. He married HATWIGATE Saxony and they had five children together. He then had two sons with ALOFR of Mercia. He married VERICA VAERICA CHLODESWINTHE Princess of Sweden of the Franks. She died at age 30 without issue. He died in 524 in Saxony, Germany, at the age of 64.

King Hulderick Hulderic Childeric Huldericus King Saxons *son of HUTUGAST HATTWIGATE King of Saxony* - **Sachsen, Germany**

When King Hulderick Hulderic Childeric Huldericus King Saxons was born in 490 in Saxony, Germany, his father, HUTUGAST, was 30. He married Queen Hathwigate von Saxony in Saxony, Germany. They had two children during their marriage. He died in 540 at the age of 50.

BUDIC Bodicus Von Wettin King of Saxony *son of King Hulderick Hulderic Childeric Huldericus King Saxons* - **Sachsen, Germany**

When BUDIC Bodicus Von Wettin King of Saxony was born in 540 in Saxony, Germany, his father, King, was 50 and his mother, Queen, was 50. He married Bodicus VonSaxony and they had four children during their marriage. He died in 568 in Saxony, Germany, at the age of 28.

Berthold VonSaxony *son of BUDIC Bodicus Von Wettin King of Saxony -* **Sachsen, Germany**

Berthold VonSaxony was born in 592 in Saxony, Germany. He married Lady Berthold Von Saxony in Saxony, Germany. They had one child during their marriage. He died in 633 in Saxony, Germany, at the age of 41.

Sighard King of Saxony *son of Berthold VonSaxony -* **Sachsen, Germany**

Sighard King of Saxony was born in 630 in Saxony, Germany, the child of Berthold. He married Julanda Von Saxony in Saxony, Germany. They had five children during their marriage. He died in 691 in Saxony, Germany, at the age of 61.

Dieteric Theodoric "King" De Saxons *son of Sighard King of Saxony* - **Sachsen, Germany**

When Dieteric Theodoric "King" De Saxons was born in April 675 in Saxony, Germany, his father, Sighard, was 45 and his mother, Julanda, was 30. He married Dobiogera VONWENDEN and they had 10 children together. He also had one son from another relationship. He died in 740 in Saxony, Germany, at the age of 65.

Wernikind Von Wettin *son of Dieteric Theodoric "King" De Saxons* - **Sachsen, Germany**

Old Saachsen

When Wernikind Von Wettin was born in 704 in Saxony, Germany, his father, Dieteric, was 29 and his mother, Dobiogera, was 32. He married Kunhilde VonRugen and they had six children together. He then had one son with GUNDELINDE DERUGEN. He died in 768 in Saxony, Germany, at 64.

When Bruno I Lord was born in 726 in Saxony, Germany, his father, Wernikind, was 22. He married Dau Assabrag in Saxony, Germany. They had two children during their marriage.

He died, along with several other Saxon noblemen, in a battle against Norsemen warriors (probably Danes of the Great Heathen Army defeated by King Alfred the Great) on 2 February 880.

The battle at Ebstorf near Lüneburg was a crushing defeat and Duke Bruno, the bishops of Minden and Hildesheim, as well as twelve Saxon counts were killed. According to the chronicler Bishop Thietmar of Merseburg, Bruno died in a flooded river, which probably took place during the battle or a retreat. He was succeeded by his younger brother Otto the Illustrious.

Made a Saint
Bruno is venerated as a saint and martyr in the Catholic Church, being honored with a feast day on 2 February under the name **St. Bruno of Saxony**. According to legend, he is the founder of Brunswick and ancestor of Count Brun I in the Derlingau, though an affiliation is uncertain.

BRUNO Saxon Ergen *son of Bruno I Lord* - **Sachsen, Germany**

When BRUNO Saxon Ergen was born in 756 in Saxony, Germany, his father, Bruno, was 30 and his mother, Dau, was 30. He married Hasalda of The Saxons in France. They had six children during their marriage. He died in 813 in Saxony, Germany, at the age of 57.

Leave Old Saxony - Sachem, Germany

It has been claimed that the Old Saxons were composed of an aristocracy of nobles, a free warrior class of distinction and renown, leading freemen united and controlled by ancient custom of kindred and clan.

> *"Social differences were jealously guarded by social prescription. The death penalty was imposed on any man who married above his rank; the marriage of a man below his station was severely condemned; bastardy was not tolerated; intermarriage between Saxons and other Germans was frowned upon; and strangers were hated. So tenaciously did the Saxons cling to their ancient customary law that clear traces of these social survivals persisted in Saxony down through the Middle Ages."*[3]

Chapter Twelve

Out of Saxony, Germany into France

Bernard 'The Dane' de Harcourt *son of BRUNO Saxon Ergen* - **Normandy, France**

Bernard - The Dane Harcourt was born in 860 in France. He married Sprote DeBourgoyne in 899 in France. They had nine children during their marriage.

Bernard, a nobleman of the blood royal of Saxony, who, being born in Denmark, was surnamed the Dane. Bernard was chief counselor, and second in command to-the famous Rollo, progenitor to the Kings of England of the Norman line, and obtained the Lordships of Harcourt.

Bernard converted to Christianity at Rouen the following year and shortly afterwards received from Rollo the county of Pont-Audemer in Roumois (today in the Eure *département*) then, later, the city of Harcourt.

He was a Viking jarl (earl) of Danish origins. After the accords of Saint-Clair-sur-Epte that officially gave birth to the duchy of Normandy in 911 he put himself in the service of another jarl, Rollo.

Under Rollo's son and successor Duke William, Bernard was charged at the beginning of the 930s with putting down the serious uprising led by a certain Riouf (a Norman from the west, who had besieged the Duke in Rouen).

Around 935 he put down a revolt in Bessin and Cotentin by Viking communities completely independent from the young and fragile power of the dukedom, unlike the east of the duchy of Normandy where its ducal power was affirmed a little later.

Later, on William's premature death by assassination, Bernard became regent of the duchy of Normandy in December 942, beside Anslech de Bricquebec, Osmond de Conteville and Raoul Taisson.

In 945-946, Bernard appealed to Harald Bluetooth and his Danes to defend the duchy when it was attacked by the Carolingian king Louis of Outremer and Hugh the Great, Duke of the Franks. Louis was attempting to retake the lands of the west in Normandy that had been granted to the Viking bands thirty years earlier. Bernard died a few years later (before 960). He is the ancestor of two great Anglo-Norman baronial families, the Beaumonts and the Harcourts.

Harcourt Castle - Eure, Haute-Normandy, France

The Château d'Harcourt, situated in Eure region of France, is a masterpiece of medieval architecture. The cradle of the Harcourt family, the castle is one of the best-preserved castles in the country and contains the oldest arboretum in France.
Although the lords of Harcourt trace their origins to the year 1000, it is only in the second half of the 12th century that the existence of a castle can be proven from historical texts. Robert II d'Harcourt was a companion in the crusade of Richard Lionheart.

The fortress appears to have seldom been under siege through history. It is only at the time of the Hundred Years' War that Harcourt became a military base. In 1418, the castle was claimed by the English, but they were eventually expelled by the counts of Dunois, Eu and Saint-Pol in 1449.

The French Wars of Religion caused an increase in defensive fortifications in the castle. In 1588, the members of a league occupied the castle. In the 17th century, the castle lost all military interest; it was then partially abandoned and invaded by vegetation after Louis Gervais Delamarre acquired it in 1802. With his death, Harcourt was bestowed to the Royal Academy of Agriculture of France.

Torfin "The Rich" de Harcourt *son of Bernard 'The Dane' de Harcourt -* **Tours, Indre-et-Loire, Centre, France**

Torfin "The Rich" de Harcourt was born in 920 in Tours, Centre, France, when his father, Bernard, was 60 and his mother, Sprote, was 40. He married Ertemberge De Brioquibec and they had 31 children together. He also had one son with Lady WEVIA Duceline de Crépon. He then married Gudrid in 1007 in Greenland. Torfin died in 1010 in Eure, Haute-Normandie, France, at the age of 90.

He was a great Norman feudal baron. He was a grandson of the Viking chiefs of Scandinavia who accompanied Rollo ABT 900 A.D. in the Norse invasion of northern France where they permanently settled and gave to the country its name "Normandy".

Torf possessed numerous lordships in Normandy, being Seigneur de Torville, Torcy, Torny, Torly, du Ponteautord, etc. He was a son of Bernard the Dane, the most powerful of the feudal nobles of Normandy during the reign of Duke William I and Regent during the minority of Duke Richard I.

Thorold Tourude Seigneur of Pont-Audemer de Harcourt *son of Torfin "The Rich" de Harcourt* - **Normandy, France**

Thorold Tourude Seigneur of Pont-Audemer de Harcourt married Sanfrie De Montfort De Crepon and they had 25 children. He then married Adeline De MONTFORT and they had three children together. He had 16 brothers and 14 sisters.

He inherited all his father's titles and became Sire du Ponte Audemer which became his principal residence and by which name he was commonly known.

By his marriage he enhanced his position among the Norman nobility, and he was a prominent figure during the reigns of Dukes Richard II, Richard III, and Robert 'the Devil' (996-1035).

Humphrey De Pontaudemer De HARCOURT (De Vielles) *son of Thorold Tourude Seigneur of Pont-Audemer de Harcourt -* **Normandie, France**

Harcourt Castle – Normandy France

When Humphrey De Pontaudemer De HARCOURT (De Vielles) was born in 980 in Eure, Haute-Normandie, France, his father, Thorold, was 52 and his mother, Sanfrie, was 44. He married Aubreye of Denmark, Duchess De Vielle, La Auberie DE LA HALE in 1005 in Harcourt, Haute-Normandie, France. They had 21 children in 42 years. He died on September 28, 1044, in Normandel, Basse-Normandie, France, at the age of 64.

He was son of Thorold de Pont-Audemer and grandson of a Torf, from whose name the village of Tourville-sur-Pont-Audemer is derived. Humphrey's mother was Duvelina, sister of Gunnora, concubine of Richard I, Duke of Normandy. Thus Humphrey and his Beaumont descendants were kinsmen of the Norman Dukes and other members of the early Anglo-Norman nobility.

Besides Beaumont-le-Roger, he had lands dispersed through the whole of Normandy, in Cotentin, in Hiémois, in the Pays d'Auge, in Basse Seine (Vatteville-la-Rue), in Évrecin (Normanville) and

220

in Vexin normand (Bouafles). These lands originated in the favor of the dukes Richard II and Robert II, from confiscated church lands. The "honor" of Beaumont was, for example, constituted from the remains of the lands of the abbey of Bernay. However, the lands around Pont-Audemer came to him by family inheritance.

In 1034, he restored the monastery at Préaux, a few kilometres from Pont-Audemer, with monks from the Saint-Wandrille.

During the minority of Duke William the Bastard, Roger I of Tosny, holder of the "honor" of Conches, attacked Humphrey's domains. But around 1040, Humphrey's son, Roger de Beaumont, met and defeated Roger in battle, during which Roger was killed.

Lady Albreda de Preaux de Harcourt *daughter of Humphrey De Pontaudemer De HARCOURT (De Vielles)* **- Normandie, France**

When Lady Albreda de Preaux de Harcourt was born in 1016 in Préaux, Basse-Normandie, France, her father, Humphrey, was 36 and her mother, Aubreye, was 32. She married Hubert DeRIE and they had 29 children together. She also married Eudes Odo FitzGeoffry Baron de Rie in France. She died in 1112 in Somme, Picardie, France, at 96.

Ranulphus dePraers *son of Lady Albreda de Preaux de Harcourt* **- Castle Rye, Normandie Province, France**

When Ranulphus dePraers, Lord of Stoke was born in 1038 his father, Hubert, was 21 and his mother was 22. He married Margaret De La Ferte Mace and they had 21 children together. He married Alice DeNewhall in 1100 in Chester, Cheshire. He died in 1127 in Nayland, Suffolk, having lived 89 years.

William the Conqueror Connection

Ranulphus de Praers, is the first ancestor of the Stokes family in England. Lord of the village of Stoke near Liverpool. Also known as the Baron of Griche in Derbyshire. He served William the Conqueror in 1066 and was granted lands in Derbyshire, Lincolnshire, Leicestershire, Staffordshire and Cheshire. He married a daughter of William de la Ferte, Lord of Weston and Stokes, near Bath, by barony from conquest of England.

Chapter Twelve

Norman Conquest of England-
The Battle of Hasting, 1066
Out of Europe, Into England

In 1066 William the Conqueror set sail from Normandy to take part in one of the fiercest battles on British soil and one that changed the course of history forever...

Following the death of Edward the Confessor (King of Anglo-Saxon England), in January 1066, Harold Godwinson was named king. Edward had been childless and so Harold, the husband of Edward's sister, was chosen to succeed him but it wasn't a popular decision with everyone.

Across the Channel there was one man who felt he had more right to the English throne and so William Duke of Normandy, a distant blood relative of the dead king, gathered his troops and crossed the water to Britain.

 What ensued on 14 October 1066 was one of the bloodiest battles in British history – famously immortalized on the **Bayeaux Tapestry** (shown here) – and saw the death of King Harold and the birth of a new ruling dynasty as the Anglo-Saxons made way for the Normans.

William Fitz Ranulf DeStoke *son of Ranulphus dePraers* - Castle Rye, Normandie Province, France

William Fitz Ranulf DeStoke was born in 1088 in Bayeux, Basse-Normandie, France. His father, Ranulphus, was 50 and his mother, Margaret, was 36.

He married Maud de Baliol in 1116 in France. They had ten children during their marriage. He died in 1121 in East Stoke, Dorset, England.

Sir Richard Knight DeStokes *son of William FitzRanulf DeStoke* - Dorset, England

When Sir Richard Knight DeStokes was born in 1118 in Dorset, his father, William, was 30 and his mother, Maud de Baldi, was 23. He had one son with Galtha in 1168. He died in 1167 in Dorset, at the age of 49.

Eustacius DeStoke *son of Sir Richard Knight DeStokes* - Dorset, England

Eustacius DeStoke was born in 1168 in Dorset, the child of Sir Richard DeStoke. He married Margaret De Englinus in 1198 in Dorset. They had one son during their marriage. Eustacius died in 1202 in Dorset, at the age of 34.

224

Eudo De Stoke *son of Eustacius DeStoke* - **East Stoke, Dorset, England**

Eudo De Stoke was born in 1199 in East Stoke, Dorset, the child of Eustacius and Margaret. He married Felicia in 1229 in Dorset. They had one child during their marriage. He died in 1236 in Dorset, at the age of 37 and is buried at St.

Mary's Church in East Stoke..

Sir William I DeStoke *son of Eudo De Stoke* - **East Stoke, Dorset, England**

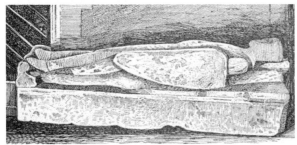

Located at St. Martin-on-the-Walls Wareham Purbeck

Sir William DeStoke was born in 1230 in East Stoke, Dorset, the child of Eudo and Felicia. He married Mathia in 1272 in Dorset. They had one child during their marriage.

He died in 1292 in East Stoke, Dorset, at the age of 62, and was buried in Wareham, Dorset.

Sir William deStoke son *of Sir William I DeStoke* - **East Stoke, Dorset, England**

Stokes

William deStoke was born in 1273 in East Stoke, Dorset, the child of Sir William and Mathia. He had one daughter with Johanna de Gouiz in 1297. He died in 1332 in East Stoke, Dorset, at the age of 59.

Sued for Fishing on Neighbor's Property

Elizabeth, who was wife of John de Burgh, brought an action against this William de Stoke, William his son, and others, for fishing in her waters in the rivers Pudele and Frome. Whereupon he pleads that those rivers run through divers vills, and every man having lands adjoining thereto is accustomed to fish therein, so far as his lands extend. That he is lord of the vill of Stoke, through which the said waters flow, and that he only fished in that part of them which adjoined his own lands, as he was well entitled to do, and not in the free fishery of the said Elizabeth.

Alice DeStoke *daughter of William deStoke* - **East Stoke, Dorset, England**

Chantmarle Coat of Arms

Alice DeStoke was born in 1297 in East Stoke, Dorset, the child of William and Johanna. She married John de Chantmarle in 1318. They had two children during their marriage. She died in East Stoke, Dorset.

In Norman French Chantmarle means "the song of the blackbird".

John Chantmarle, II *son of Alice DeStoke* - **Chantmarle Manor, Frome Valley,**

Chantmarle Manor

When John Chantmarle was born in 1318 his father, John, was 23 and his mother, Alice, was 21. He married Johanna in 1357 in Vendée, Pays de la Loire, France. They had one child during their marriage. John died in 1358 at the age of 40

Walter Chantmarle *son of John Chantmarle* - **Chantmarle Manor, Frome Valley, England**

Walter Chantmarle was born in 1345 the child of John and Johanna. He married Alice Micheldever. They had one child during their marriage.

John III Chantmarle *son of Walter Chantmarle* - **Chantmarle Manor, Frome Valley, England**

John Chantmarle III was born in 1370 the child of Walter and Alice. He had one son and two daughters with Mrs NN Chantmarle in 1418.

Ghost Story
For many years a ghost had been reportedly heard in the Great Hall to repeat three times "Search for Wat Perkins!" This occurred on the same night each year. Then one day two workmen clearing a ditch found a headless skeleton.

Following an investigation a widow living at nearby "Kit Whistle" cottage confessed to the murder of a Scottish peddler some 22 years before. She had buried his head under the cottages hearthstone and disposed of the body in the ditch. It is said that after her arrest the ghost was never heard from again.

Christie Chantmarle *daughter of John Chantmarle III* - **Staffordshire, England**

Christie Chantmarle was born in 1418 at the family estate in the Frome Valley. She married and had one son and two daughters with John Jordaine. She then married Thomas Jordaine and they had two children together. Christie passed away at age 37.

The Jordaine family came originally from Italy into southern France, then England and were very prominent in society in the 1400 and 1500's.
The Jordans left the Catholic Church to join the reformation,. They worshiped secretly in barns, homes, and other places that they could feel safe for if they were caught – the punishment was death. Many suffered presecution by the Catholic Church.

Robert JORDAINE. *son of Christie Chantmarle* - **Melcombe Regis, Dorset, England**

When Robert JORDAINE. was born in 1455 in Melcombe Regis, Dorset, his father, Thomas, was 37 and his mother, Christie, was 37. He married Christie CHANTMARLE. in 1479 in France. They had one child during their marriage. He died in 1500 at the age of 45.

The port of Melcombe Regis is famous for at least two reasons: First, Melcombe Regis, now known as Weymouth, was one of the first points of entry of the Black Death into England in the summer of 1348. Infected soldiers and sailors returning from the Hundred Years' War, or perhaps rats from a visiting spice ship possibly carried the disease there. No one knows for certain.

Secondly, The ship *Abigail* set sail from Weymouth in 1628 with many Dorset emigrants bound for New England. This particular passage was important as it carried the new government for the London Plantation in Massachusetts i.e: the first Governor of Massachusetts, John Endicott.

Perhaps most importantly, **it carried the John Burbank, the connection to "Olive Branch" (Olive Soule) of George "Mayflower" Soule's line, to the New World.**

Robert Jordaine II *son of Robert JORDAINE.* - **Regis, Dorset, England**

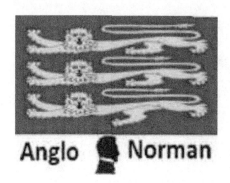

Robert Jordaine II was born in 1470 in Dorset, the child of Robert and Christie. He married his wife Anne in 1499 at Melcombe Regis, Dorset. They had four children in 40 years. He died in 1540 in Melcombe Regis, Dorset, at the age of 70.

Robert Jordaine III *son of Robert Jordaine* - **Melcombe Regis, Dorset, England**

When Robert Jordaine was born in 1500 in Melcombe Regis, Dorset, his father, Robert, was 30 and his mother was 20. He married Jane Coker in Melcombe Regis, Dorset. They had 14 children. He died on October 12, 1589, in Melcombe Regis, Dorset, having lived a long life of 89 years.

Thomas Jordan *son of Robert III Jordaine* - **Melcombe, Dorset, England**

When Thomas Jordan was born in 1533 his father, Robert, was 33 and his mother, Jane, was 29. He married Agnes Burte on June 20, 1547, in Tarrant Hinton, Dorset. They had eight children in 49 years. He died on July 8, 1589, in London, London, at the age of 56.

Thomas Jordan Jr. *son of Thomas Jordan* - **Denham, Suffolk, England**

When Thomas Jordan was born in 1560 his father, Thomas, was 28 and his mother, Agnes, was 30.

He married Mart Wilkinson in 1588. He died on November 6, 1599, at the age of 39 and is buried at St. John's Church in Woodbridge, Suffolk,.

Chapter Thirteen

Migration to America

Stephen Jordan *son of Thomas Jordan* - **Denham, Suffolk, England**

When Stephen Jordan was born in 1589 his father, Thomas, was 29 and his mother, Mary, was 29. He married Susannah Peabody on April 12, 1610. They had nine children in 33 years. He died on August 2, 1669, in Newbury, Massachusetts, having lived a long life of 80 years.

Joane Ann Jordan *daughter of Stephen Jordan* - **Denham, Suffolk, England**

Immigration to America from England

When Joane Ann Jordan was born in 1618 her father, Stephen, was 29 and her mother, Susannah, was 33. She married John Burbank in 1631.

In 1635 John Burbank and wife Ann Jordan, who were servants to George Hadborne (glove maker), came to America aboard the "Abigail." Coming, as they did, as

233

servants or "subsidy men" was the custom in those early days. It usually took about four years to pay off the indenture, which accounts for the time between their living in Charlestown and later Hampton, NH, and their arriving at Rowley.

After settling in Rowley, Massachusetts they had five children in 15 years. Joane died a young mother in February 1641 in Rowley, Massachusetts at the age of 31. He then married Jemima Burbank and they had four children together. He died on April 10, 1683, in Rowley, Massachusetts, having lived a long life of 83 years.

In 1643 John is recorded as owning "the seventh lot" on Bradford Street in "Rogers Plantation, now Rowley, MA. The records read. . ."To John Burbank, one lott containinge an acree and a halfe, bounded on the south side by Thomas Summer's house lott, part of it lyinge on the west side, and part of it on the east side of the streete." In 1672 he owned some fresh meadow on Plum Island.

John Burbank subscribed to the freeman's oath on May 13, 1640, which would be an indication that he was a member in good standing in the Puritan faith (Congregational).

John Burbank Jr. *son of Joane Ann Jordan* - **Rowley, Massachusetts**

When John Burbank Jr. was born on May 13, 1640, in Rowley, Massachusetts, his father, John, was 26 and his mother, Joane, was 22. He was married three times and had five sons and four daughters. He died on June 1, 1709, in Suffield, Connecticut, at the age of 69, and was buried at the Old Center Cemetery there.

TIMOTHY Burbank *son of John Burbank* - **Haverhill, Essex Co., MA**

When Timothy Burbank was born on May 30, 1668, in Haverhill, Massachusetts, his father, John, was 28 and his mother, Susannah, was 28.

When he was twelve years old his father moved to Suffield CT but left Timothy to live with Capt. Nathaniel Saltonstall of Ipswich probably as an apprentice to become a mariner. He sailed out of Salem at first but around 1698 he settled in Boston. At one time he served as captain of the brigantine, *Swallow*, a ship of 25 tons.

He married Rebecca Darling Burbank on July 3, 1695. They had six children in 16 years. He died at sea September 1706, at the age of 38.

Timothy Burbank Jr. *son of* Timothy *Burbank* - **Salem, Essex, Massachusetts**

When Timothy Burbank, a blacksmith, was born on October 13, 1703, in Salem, Massachusetts, his father, Timothy, was 35 and his mother, REBECCA, was 28.

He married Mary Kempton on December 12, 1728 in Plymouth, Massachusetts where they had 12 children together. He died on October 13, 1793, in Plymouth, Massachusetts, at the age of 90, and was buried there.

Ezra Burbank *son of Timothy Burbank* - **Plymouth, Massachusetts**

When Ezra Burbank was born on February 20, 1738, in Plymouth, Massachusetts, his father, Timothy, was 34 and his mother, Mary, was 30.

He married Priscilla SAVERY on February 13, 1762, in Plymouth, Massachusetts. He then married Mrs. Polly Burbank and they had one son together. He died on February 25, 1800, in Plymouth, Massachusetts, at the age of 62, and was buried atop Burial Hill next to the site of the fort that protected Plymouth Harbor from 1621 until 1676.

David Burbank - *son of Ezara Burbank* - **Plymouth, Massachusetts**

David Burbank was born in 1805 in Plymouth, Massachusetts, and the child of Polly. He married **Olive Soule** on November 22, 1829, in his hometown. He was a rope maker at the famous Plymouth Cordage Co.

They had six children in 13 years. He died on February 16, 1855, in Plymouth, Massachusetts, of Scrofula or King's Evil (a tuberous growth on the neck) at the age of 48 years, 7 months and is buried at Plymouth's famous Burial Hill.

David Winslow Burbank - *son of David Burbank and Olive Soule -1807 – 1878) - daughter of Asaph Soule* - Plymouth, Massachusetts

David W Burbank was born in April 1835 in Plymouth, Massachusetts. In 1860 he married Sarah Holmes Lakin and they had one daughter, Susan Porter. He rose to the rank of Sergeant in the Union Army during the Civil War.

He was a shoemaker and died in 1900 at the age of 65 and is buried at Cedar Grove Cemetery in Dorchester, Massachusetts.

David W Burbank, the son of Olive Soule, was born in April 1835 in Plymouth, Massachusetts. George "Mayflower" Soule is David's 7th great grandfather

From George "Mayflower" Soule to David Winslow Burbank

John Soule (1632 - 1707) *son of George "Mayflower Compact" Soule*

Benjamin Soule (1665 - 1729) *son of John Soule*

Ebenezer Soule (1710 - 1792) *son of Benjamin Soule*

Asaph Soule (1739 - 1823) *son of Ebenezer Soule*

Asaph Soule (1779 - 1812) *son of Asaph Soule*

Olive Soule (1807 - 1878) *daughter of Asaph Soule*

David Winslow Burbank (1835 - 1908) *son of Olive Soule*

What Happened to the Mayflower?

Perhaps the answer lies in England midway between London and Oxford, in the small village of Jordans in the South Buckinghamshire countryside. It is there where you will find what locals, for centuries, have been calling the "Mayflower Barn." The farm on which it is located's name dates back into the late Middle Ages. Its known history begins in 1618 when Thomas Russell bought it.

"Mayflower Barn" Jordan, Buckinghamshire, England

Part of the present farmhouse was already there when Russell added to it in 1624. At the same time he also built a substantial new main barn with timbers bought from a shipbreaker's yard in Rotherhithe. Oral history records the barn as being constructed with timbers salvaged from the *Mayflower*, the same *Mayflower* that carried the Pilgrim Fathers to Plymouth and the New World.

Researcher Dr Rendel Harris early in the twentieth century confirmed that the beams were definitely from a ship and that a central beam had cracked and been repaired - consistent with an event recorded as occurring during that historic voyage.

Letters carved roughly on another beam could, it was suggested, be all that is left of "Mayflower, Harwich."

In the dining room of the original farmhouse is an old elm door reckoned to be from a ship's cabin. It is strengthened with oak batons and carved with a floral pattern. Could the carving be a hawthorn or "Mayflower," and the door another link with the Pilgrim Fathers' famous vessel?

Door from the Mayflower?

The well-preserved barn was a popular tourist attraction, receiving visitors each year from all over the world and particularly from the Americas but is now privately owned and not opened to the public.

Chapter Fourteen

Famous Relatives

The extensive list of our famous relatives that follow is only through our connection to Charlemagne and William the Conqueror. This is only a partial listing of those notables in theses lines and includes only those names most likely to be familiar to the reader.

The listing of connections to royalty would be much too extensive to list. As it could include:

- Every French monarch from Louis I (except 3),
- Every English monarch since 1040 (except Harold II),
- Every Scottish monarch from 1097 forward –
- Essentially every monarch of Ireland dating from before the Christian era, BC

You have already gone through scores of royal personages to arrive at this point so there is no need to belabor the royalty point.

We are following primarily through:

Alice de Harcourt, Charlemagne's, 11th Great grand daughter and of Thorold Tourude Seigneur of Pont-Audemer de Harcourt

William the Conqueror via his grandmother Doda 'Duxia', Princess-Scotland De Scotland (973 - 1003) *daughter of King of Scotland Malcolm II*

Odin Woden Frithuwaldsson - All of the Anglo-Saxon and Scandinavian Kings trace their direct male ancestry to Odin.

U.S. Presidents and Their Ladies

George Washington - *1st U.S. President*

1) **John Adams** – *2ⁿᵈ U.S. President*

> **Abigail (Smith) Adams** - *First Lady of President John Adams*

2) **Thomas Jefferson** – *2ⁿᵈ ·U.S. President*
3) **James Madison** - *4th U.S. President*
4) **George Clinton** - *4th U.S. Vice President*
5) **James Monroe** – *5ᵗʰ U.S. President*
6) **John Quincy Adams** - *6th U.S. President*
7) **William Harrison** – *9ᵗʰ U.S. President*
8) **Zachary Taylor** - *12th U.S. President*

> **Lucretia (Rudolph) Garfield** - *First Lady of President James Garfield*

9) **Franklin Pierce** – *14th U.S. President*
10) **Rutherford B. Hayes** – *19ᵗʰ U.S. President*
11) **Grover Cleveland** - *22nd and 24th U.S. President*
12) **Benjamin Harrison** – *23ʳᵈ U.S. President*

> **Lou (Henry) Hoover** - *First Lady of President Herbert Hoover*

> **Ellen Louise (Axon) Wilson** - *First Lady of President Woodrow Wilson*

13) **Theodore Roosevelt** - *26th U.S. President*
14) **William Howard Taft** - *27th U.S. President*
15) **James Sherman** - *27th U.S. Vice-President*
16) **Warren G. Harding** – *29ᵗʰ U.S. President*
17) **Calvin Coolidge** - *30th U.S. President*
18) **Herbert Hoover** – *31ˢᵗ U.S. President*
19) **Franklin D. Roosevelt** - *32nd U.S. President*

> **Eleanor Roosevelt** - *First Lady of President Franklin D. Roosevelt*

20) **Harry S. Truman** – *33ʳᵈ U.S. President*

> **Edith (Bolling) Wilson** - *First Lady of President Woodrow Wilson*

Mamie (Doud) Eisenhower - *First Lady of President Dwight Eisenhower*

21) **Richard Nixon** – *37th U.S. President*

22) **Gerald Ford** - *38th U.S. President*

23) **Jimmy Carter** - *39th U.S. President*

   Nancy Reagan – *First Lady of Ronald Regan*

24) **George H. W. Bush** - *41st U.S. President*

25) **Nelson Rockefeller** – *41st U.S. Vice President*

   Barbara (Pierce) Bush - *First Lady of President George H.W. Bush*

26) **William Jefferson Blythe, III a/k/a "Bill" Clinton** – *42nd U.S. President*

27) **President George W. Bush** - *43rd U.S. President*

28) **Barack Obama** – *44th U.S. President*

Wow! More than half of our presidents are on the tree

American Leaders

Alexander Hamilton - *1st U.S. Secretary of the Treasury*

Dick Cheney – *46th U. S. Vice President*

Adlai Stevenson III - *U.S. Senator from Illinois*

William Rufus Day - *36th U.S. Secretary of State*

Howard Dean - *79th Governor of Vermont, Presidential candidate*

John Foster Dulles - *52nd U.S. Secretary of State*

Sarah Palin - *9th Governor of Alaska – Vice Presidential candidate*

Sandra Day O'Connor - *First Female U.S. Supreme Court Justice*

Jeb Bush - *43rd Governor of Florida*

Mitt Romney – *Massachusetts Governor and U. S. presidential candidate*

John McCain – *U. S. Senator and presidential candidate*

Joseph P. Kennedy III - *U.S. Congressman, grandson of JFK*

Mike Huckabee – *44th governor of Arkansas and Presidential candidate*

Confederate Generals

General Robert Edward Lee - *Confederate Army - U.S. Civil War*
General James Longstreet - *Confederate Army - U.S. Civil War*

US Pioneers

Susan B. Anthony - *Women's Rights Advocate*
Harriet Beecher Stowe – *Abolitionist and author "Uncle Tom's Cabin"*
Sally Ride - *1st American Woman in Space*
Captain Meriwether Lewis - *Lewis and Clark Expedition*
Helen Keller - *Author and Activist*
Admiral Richard Byrd - *Polar Explorer - first to reach the North Pole*
Alan Bartlett Shepard Jr. - *Mercury and Apollo Astronaut*

U.S. Patriots

Roger Sherman - *Signer of the Declaration of Independence*
Caesar Rodney - *Signer of the Declaration of Independence*
Thomas Nelson *Signer of the Declaration of Independence*
William Floyd - *Signer of the Declaration of Independence*
Pierce Butler - *Signer of the Declaration of Independence*
Robert Treat Paine - *Signer of the Declaration of Independence*
John Hancock - *Signer of the Declaration of Independence*
Nicholas Gilman - *Signer of the U.S. Constitution*
George Mason - *Father of the U.S. Bill of Rights*
Patrick Henry - *"Give me liberty, or give me death!"*
Samuel Prescott - *Completed Paul Revere's Midnight Ride*
Francis Scott Key - *Author of "The Star Spangled Banner"*
Samuel Howard - *Boston Tea Party Participant*
General George S. Patton - *U.S. Army - World War II*
Commodore Matthew C. Perry - *Led Black Ships Expedition to Japan*
Oliver Hazard Perry - *Hero of Lake Erie during the War of 1812*
General Douglas MacArthur - *U.S. Army - World War II*
Benjamin Spock – *Pediatrician*

Inventors, Scientists

Eli Whitney - *Inventor of the Cotton Gin*
Charles Darwin - *Theory of Evolution, Founder of Biology*
Wernher von Braun - *Rocket scientist*
Sir Francis Bacon – *One of the founders of science*
Margaret Mead – *Cultural anthropologist, author and speaker*

Infamous Relatives

Rev. George Burroughs - *Executed for Witchcraft, Salem 1692*
Major John Pitcairn - *British Commander at Battle of Lexington*
Lizzie Borden - *Accused Murderess*
Lee Harvey Oswald - *Accused Assassin of President John F. Kennedy*
G. Gordon Libby – *Watergate burglar*
Fletcher Christian – *leader of the Mutiny on the "Bounty"*
Anthony Blunt – *Soviet spy*
Patty Hearst – *Kidnap victim – Joined the Symbionese Liberation Army*
Countess Elizabeth Bathory – *1600s Mass murderer (Estimated 650+ victims)*
Che Guevera – *Communist revolutionist*
Hermann Goering – *Nazi leader, president of the Reichstag*
Manfred von Richtofen – *"The Red Baron" WWI German fighter pilot with 80 kills*
Rob Roy McGregor – *1700s "Scottish Robin Hood"*
Jezebel – Of biblical fame

Norse Gods and Godesses

Frigg
Thor
Odin Woden
Baldr
Godwulf of Geat
Gefion of Godwulf - godess

Biblical Figures

Abraham
Noah
Methuselah
Joseph of Nazereth
Jezebel
Josiah
David
Pope John XII – 964
Jacob
Joseph – Coat of Many Colors

Popes

Pope Benedict VII – 983
Pope Gregory V – 999
Pope Benedict VIII – 1024
Pope John XIX – 1032
Pope St Leo IX – 1054
Pope Benedict IX – 11th century
Pope Stephen IX - 1058
Pope Calixtus II – 1124
Pope Amadeus VIII – 1449
Pope Paul III – 1468
Pope Leo X – 1475
Pope Leo XI – 1535
Pope Benedict XIII – 1649

Royal Connections –.

This list could include:
- Every French monarch from Louis I (except 3),
- Every English monarch since 1040 (except Harold II),
- Every Scottish monarch from 1097 forward –
- Essentially every monarch of Ireland dating from before the Christian era, BC
- Every Scandanavian Royal

Royal Connections (Continued)

A few worthy of note:

Odin – *From whom all of European royalty is decended*
King Solomon – *The Wisdom of Solomon*
Charlemagne – *First Holy Roman Emperor*
William the Conqueror -
Helen of Troy – *Her beauty launched a thousand shipsAnne*
Boleyn - *2nd Wife of King Henry VIII*
Jane Seymour - *3rd Wife of King Henry VIII*
Princess Diana - *Princess of Wales, wife of Prince Charles*
Sara Ferguson – *Wife of Prince Andrew*
Queen Elizabeth II - *Queen of the United Kingdom*
Prince William - *Duke of Cambridge*
Sarah Ferguson - *Duchess of York*
Catherine Elizabeth (Kate) Middleton - *Duchess of Cambridge*
Prince George - *Prince of Cambridge*
Ivan the Terrible – *First Czar of Russia*
Napoleon Bonaparte - *Emperor of the French*
Marie Antoinette – *Beheaded wife of King Lois XVI of France*
Archduke Franz Ferdinand of Austria - *Assassinated 1914 (which started WW1).*

Show Business Folk

William Bradley Pitt a/k/a "Brad Pitt" - *Actor*
Vincent Price - *Actor*
Marilyn Monroe - *Actress, Model, and Singer*
Raquel Welch - *Actress*
Humphrey Bogart - *Movie Actor*
Tom Hanks - *Actor*
Ron Howard – *Movie director*
Christopher Reeve - *Actor*
Walt Disney - *Co-Founder of The Walt Disney Company*
Katharine Hepburn - *Movie Actress*
Jodie Foster – *Actress*
Laura Dern – *Actress*
Angelina Jolie - *Actress*
Brooke Shields – *Actress*
Halle Berry - *Actress*

Show Business Folk (Continued)

Ellen DeGeneres - *Comedian, actress and talk show host*
Fay Ray - *Movie Actress*
Steve McQueen – *Actor*
Lee Marvin – *Actor*
Sissy Spacek – *Actress*
Cindy Crawford - *Model*
Clint Eastwood - *Actor*
Marlon Brando – *Actor*
Matt Damon – *Actor*
Roy Rogers – *Cowboy actor, singer*
Hugh Grant - *Actor*
Lucille Ball – *Actress and comedian*
Pete Seeger - *American Folk Singer*
Linda Ronstadt - *Singer*
Dick Clark - *Radio and TV Host*
Johnny Carson - *TV Host - "The Tonight Show"*
Anderson Cooper - *Television Journalist*
Orson Welles - *Radio, Stage, and Movie Actor*
Paris Hilton - *celebrity*
Bing Crosby - *Singer and Movie Actor*
Anderson Cooper – *TV commentator*
Walter Cronkite – *Broadcaster*
Ted Dawson – *Actor of "Cheers" fame*

Authors, Artists, Poets and Playwrights

William Shakespeare – *Playwright and poet*
Tolstoy - *Writer*
Jack London - *Author of "The Call of the Wild"*
Ralph Waldo Emerson - *American Poet*
Louisa May Alcott – *Novelist "Little Woman"*
Robert Frost – *Poet*
Robert Louis Stevenson – *Novelist and writer*
Norman Rockwell - *American Artist*
Albert Schweitzer – *Theologian, organist, philosopher, and physician*
Oscar Wilde – *Playwright, author and wit*
Tennessee Williams - *Playwright*
Ernest Hemingway – *Novelist and writer*

Alice Liddell - *Creator of "Alice in Wonderland"*
W. Somerset Maugham – *Writer*
F. Scott Fitzgerald – *Writer*
Laura Ingalls Wilder - *Author of "Little House on the Prairie"*
Marquis de Sade – *Erotic writer*
Sir Walter Scott - *Novelist, playwright and poet, wrote :Ivanhoe"*
T. S. Eliot – *Poet*
Helen Keller – *Both deaf and blind author and activist.*
Alfred Lord Tennyson - *Poet*
George Orwell – *Writer*
Frank Lloyd Wright - *American Architect*
John D. Rockefeller – *World's richest man in the 1800s*
Andrew Wyeth – *Painter*

Mayflower Passengers on the Author's Family Tree

I am told that if you are related to any of the Mayflower passengers listed below, then this information applies to you as well. Why? Because the book's author is related to all on the list and it's his families' lines that are followed here. Therefore, because we share common ancestry, we are related and this information applies to you as well.

William Mullins, Wife Alice Mullins + son Joseph
John Alden , Wife Priscilla Mullins Alden
Governor William Bradford –
Myles Standish, Wife Rose
George Soule
William Brewster, Wife Mary **(Wentworth)**
Mary Chilton
John Howland
Elizabeth, Tilley
Edward Doty
Richard Warren
Stephen Hopkins, Wife Elizabeth and 4 children
John Clark (MASTER'S MATE of the Mayflower)
Richard More

Other Books by Ted Burbank

- **A Guide to Plymouth's Famous Burial Hill** – Stories from beneath the gravestone
  Includes an Index and map of headstone locations

- **The Golden Age of Piracy on Cape Cod and in New England** – *How New England became the pirate's headquarters, where treasure has and still might be found in New England*

- **Cape Cod Shipwrecks** - "*Graveyard of the Atlantic*" More than 3,500 wrecks have been recorded off Cape Cod

- **A Guide to Haunted Lighthouses of New England** – *plus haunted ships, forts, ghost ships and more*

- **Shipwrecks, Pirates and Treasure in Maine** – Identifies the location of *America's first naval defeat, tales of shiprecks, pirates and their treasure.*

- **The "Islands" of Ocean Bluff and Brant Rock** – *Home of many American firsts*

- **Put it Down! Go Out and Play** or *How to have fun without TV or Computers* 365 Classic Games and activities

- ***A Homeowner's Complete Guide to Energy Independence*** or *How we eliminated our fuel and utility bills and attained "Zero Net Energy"*

- ***How to Cook Bait*** – *A cookbook for the unlucky fisherman.* Don't let the title fool you; the cookbook contains 126 really delicious recipes.

Any of these books can be ordered from Salty Pilgrim Press by going to *www.SaltyPilgrim.com*

Printed in Great Britain
by Amazon

27131018R00155